T0285233

# THE UNSEEN FALKLANDS WAR

NICK VAN DER BIJL

AMBERLEY

*I wish to dedicate this book to my wife, Penny, and our daughter, Imogen.*

First published 2022

Amberley Publishing
The Hill, Stroud
Gloucestershire, GL5 4EP

www.amberley-books.com

British Library Cataloguing in Publication Data.

A catalogue record for this book is available from the British Library.

ISBN 978 1 3981 0163 0 (print)
ISBN 978 1 3981 0164 7 (ebook)

Typesetting by SJmagic DESIGN SERVICES, India.
Printed in the UK.

# Contents

|  | Acknowledgement | 4 |
| Chapter 1 | Historical Background | 5 |
| Chapter 2 | Operation *Rosario*: 'Recovery' of Falklands (2 April) and Seizure of South Georgia (3 April) | 15 |
| Chapter 3 | Occupation of the Falklands | 28 |
| Chapter 4 | Operation *CORPORATE* | 34 |
| Chapter 5 | The Argentine Defence and Falklands Occupation | 42 |
| Chapter 6 | Approach to Battle | 57 |
| Chapter 7 | Operation *Sutton*: Landings at San Carlos Water | 70 |
| Chapter 8 | The Break-Out From San Carlos Water | 86 |
| Chapter 9 | The Advance to Stanley – 1 to 10 June | 104 |
| Chapter 10 | Capture of Stanley | 117 |
| Chapter 11 | Surrender of Argentine Ambitions in the South Atlantic | 123 |
|  | Bibliography | 128 |

# Acknowledgement

This book is designed to support an account of the 1982 Falkland War with pictorial representation. Copyright has not always been possible because cameras were removed from prisoners of war as items of intelligence interest. In 1982, I sent captured Argentine documents, maps and charts to the Ministry of Defence and was content to accept material offered of no further value to the Ministry. I deposited some images to the Imperial War Museum and the Military Intelligence Museum.

As always, it is pleasure to be able to thank several people. In particular, my wife Penny for her patience and proofreading skills; Alejandro Amendolara, a good friend in Argentina with some interesting connections; Chris Baxter, who commanded the Raiding Squadron, Royal Marines; Mr Eric Goss was the Goose Green Farm Manager; Major Gerald Cheek, the former Falklands Director of Aviation and Falkland Island Defence Force, taken prisoner and also held as internee for several weeks; Colonel Giles Orpen-Smellie was the 3rd Parachute Regiment Intelligence Officer; Nicci Pugh was a member of the Queen Alexandra's Royal Naval Nursing Service and wrote an account of her experiences in her book *White Ship - Red Crosses*; and Tom Priestley was a colleague in the HQ 3 Commando Brigade Intelligence Section.

# Chapter 1

# Historical Background

In 1592, the highly experienced Elizabethan navigator, John Davis, was 8,000 miles from England and heading toward the Straits of Magellan around South America when he is thought to have sighted the Falkland Islands. Nearly a century later, the English privateer John Strong named the channel between the two main islands after Anthony Carey, 5th Viscount Falkland and First Lord of the Admiralty.

The Falklands is an archipelago of two large islands and 776 smaller ones collectively about the size of Wales surviving the South Atlantic climate. After Captain George Anson returned from his epic circumnavigation in 1745 and recommended a station be established in the South Atlantic to counter Spanish domination, Commodore John Byron, grandfather of the poet, raised the Union flag on West Falkland in 1765. He was unaware the previous year, French sailors from St Malo had settled at Port Louis on East Falkland and when a British ship and a French ship met, both demanded surrender. Commentators such as Dr Samuel Johnson questioned the need to colonize such a place he described as,

> An island thrown aside for human life, stormy in winter and barren in winter, an island which not even the southern savages have dignified with habitations.

Five years later, the Spanish Viceroyalty of the Rio de la Plata and the French ejected the British, however Louis XV of France advised Charles III of Spain that he would not support war with Great Britain. Spain then returned West Falkland. Three years later under orders, Lieutenant Samuel Clayton RN, the garrison commander, abandoned the settlement and ordered the shipwright on HMS *Endurance* to hammer a lead plaque on the fort gates declaring:

> Be it known to all nations, that Falkland Island, with this Fort, Stonehouse, Wharf, Harbour, Bays and Creeks thereunto belonging, are the Sole Right of His Most Sacred Majesty George III, King of England, France and Ireland, Defender of the Faith etc. In witness whereof this plate is set up, and his Britannic Majesty's colours left flying as a mark of possession.

The interesting aspect of this statement is Falkland Island in the singular. Captain James Cook claimed South Georgia and South Sandwich Islands for Great Britain during his circumnavigation.

The Spanish provinces that merged to form Argentina on 9 July 1819 formed the Military Command of the *Malvinas*, the Spanish title inherited from the French *Malouines*. Four years later Argentina proclaimed sovereignty over the Falklands and built a fort on East Falkland. Great Britain insisted the claim only applied to the 'Province of Buenos Aires' and after Argentine administrators landed in 1829, appointed Luis Vernet, an adventurer from the city-state of Hamburg, to govern the colony. His arrest of three American seal-hunting ships in 1831 led to an early example of US intervention when the sloop USS *Lexington,* which was part of the US Brazil Squadron, bombarded the settlement, evacuated most of the settlers and declared the islands to be free from government. Meanwhile, Great Britain, a growing imperial power, recognised the strategic value of Cape Horn in South America and the Cape of Good Hope in southern Africa and in 1833, Captain John Onslow RN raised the Union Jack.

A British governor, assisted by a civil service and an elected legislature and executive, has administered the Falklands since – except for three and half months in 1982. The sheltered bay of Port Stanley was nominated as the capital. The governor has been Commander-in-Chief of the volunteer militia since 1847. The settlers, nicknamed 'kelpers' from the long strands of kelp around the coast, developed sheep farms throughout the 'camp', a word derived from the Spanish word *'campo'*, which translates as 'countryside'. Some families can trace their heritage to the early settlers. The 'Recovery of Las *Malvinas*' from Great Britain was first mentioned in Argentine politics in 1850. As was customary throughout the British Empire, the Falkland Islands Company was formed in 1851 to manage land and resources.

By the early twentieth century, Argentina had developed into a sophisticated nation that hosted the only overseas branch of Harrods of London. The defeat of the Royal Navy South Atlantic Squadron at the Battle of Coronel by the German Navy off the Chilean coast in November 1914 exposed the strategic vulnerability of the South Atlantic region. The defeat was avenged five weeks later at the Battle of the Falklands. The defeat of Germany in 1918 saw growing German support and several military coups in the 1920s and 1930s.

The British Territory of South Georgia and Sandwich Islands South Georgia, created in 1908, was governed by the Foreign & Commonwealth Office through the Falklands Governor and is managed by the Magistrate with British Antarctic Survey at Grytviken. Argentina had made its first claim in 1927 when it was leased a whaling station by Great Britain until 1938. Argentina then claimed it and the South Sandwich Islands.

The Second World War saw an Argentine Navy captain suggest to Congress in 1941 that since Great Britain was otherwise occupied, there was an opportunity to 'recover' the Falklands. This led in March 1942 to Operation *Tabaran* in which 1,500 troops and two ships were despatched to the Falklands. After the United Nations emerged in 1945, Argentina persisted with 'Recovery' but negotiations with Great Britain made little headway. In 1960, the Admiralty strengthened the defence with the Royal Marines Detachment. Within six years, it was renamed Naval Party 8901 (NP 8901) and based at Moody Brook Barracks. In 1972, the *Lineas Aereas del Estado* (LADE, State Airline) financed the airstrip at Stanley. The Argentine Consul was usually an Air Force officer and believed to be a front for intelligence collection. By 1974, regular flights were being flown between the Falklands and southern Argentina.

Colonel Juan Peron, a major player in Argentine politics, was first elected President in 1946 and introduced a policy of industrialization and government intervention that was neither capitalism nor communism. But after his charismatic first wife Evita died in 1952, his authoritarianism grew and when his second wife Isabel was elected President in July 1974, the internal security of Argentina and several South and Central American governments crumbled in the face of left-wing guerrillas, urban terrorism and rural subversion. Within the year, the USA persuaded eight countries to share intelligence in Operation *Condor*. The next year, Lieutenant-General Jorge Videla seized power in the First Military Junta and imposed the National Reorganization Process to address the insecurity. Meanwhile in 1976, when Lord Shackleton confirmed the economic viability of the Falklands in his Parliamentary report, the Junta severed diplomatic links with Great Britain and annexed Southern Thule, which it first claimed in 1938. It was defended by a Project Alpha of small clandestine units tasked to support Argentine territorial claims. When in 1977, cost savings saw the Labour government withdraw a task force sent to eject the Argentines, this encouraged the Junta to the keep the 'Recovery' of the Falklands and South Georgia high on the national agenda. When Mrs Margaret Thatcher was elected Prime Minister in 1979 and sought government savings, the Foreign & Commonwealth Office proposed that several small colonies be passed to claimants, such as Belize to Guatemala and the Falkland Islands to Argentina, which was not well received. In the Falklands, 1,800 Islanders voted to remain British. Ministry of Defence savings in 1982 included decommissioning the Ice Patrol Ship HMS *Endurance*.

The Military Junta ordered that a highly secret Working Committee consisting of Major-General Osvaldo Garcia (Commander Fifth Corps), Vice-Admiral Juan Lombardo (South Atlantic Theatre of Operations at Navy Headquarters) and Brigadier Sigfrido Plessel (Argentine Air Force) develop a plan to restore a territory occupied by the UK as Operation *Azul* (Blue). The aim was to conduct an operation to occupy and defend the Falklands, South Georgia and the South Sandwich Islands. An intelligence source was military *Líneas Aéreas del Estado* (LADE) airline that regularly flew to the Falkland Islands. Its office was in Stanley. Conclusions included:

- While the Falklands population regarded themselves as British, hostility was not expected and therefore establishing cordial relations by respecting lives, livelihoods, possessions, customs and human rights and the standard of living was essential when assimilating Argentine economic practices, law and culture.
- Choices for the population: 1) leave; 2) remain under Argentine governance; 3) settle elsewhere in Argentina; 4) replace the population with one of Argentine origin; 5) mandatory or voluntary Argentine nationality.

The 'Recovery' was initially decided to be 15 October because the Southern Hemisphere summer weather was predictable. During the planning, a fortnight was assessed to be necessary to assemble landing forces and 15 May emerged as D-Day as the last day suitable for the prevailing winter atmospheric conditions. The Second Junta preferred 25 May because it commemorated the 1810 Revolution Day when middle- and upper-middle-class citizens rebelled against the Spanish-controlled government.

In 1979, the young Argentine businessman Constantino Davidoff had won a contract with Christian Salvesen to dismantle the derelict whaling stations on South Georgia and shortly before Christmas 1980, he advised the British Embassy that he intended to reconnoitre the project.

By 1981, the National Reorganization Process had evolved into the chaos of revolving doors of Armed Forces officers forming Juntas. The reputation of Argentina was questioned, the economy collapsed and inflation was rampant. Oppressive internal security measures saw thousands sent to brutal interrogation centres and 11,000 people 'disappeared', some thrown from aircraft into the River Plate and Atlantic Ocean. In December, General Leopoldo Galtieri, a former Engineer and the Army commander, the hardline Admiral Jorge Anaya and Brigadier-General Basilio Lami Dozo, the Air Force commander, formed the Third Junta. Anaya had been the Naval Attache at the Argentine Embassy in London in the 1960s but his dislike of the British and refusal to learn English saw him isolated. Anaya convinced Galtieri that Argentina could regain her influence and pride and 'Recover' the Falklands using the 'coercive diplomacy' developed by India during her annexation of Goa from Portugal in 1961. Galtieri agreed and issued National Strategic Directive No. 1/82 (*Malvinas* Case) for the 'the Administration of the *Malvinas*, South Georgia and South Sandwich Islands be under a military governor appointed by the Military Committee to exercise the executive, legislative and judicial authority'. The aim was to consolidate Argentine sovereignty and develop influence in the South Atlantic. The 'Recovery' was named Operation *Rosario* (Rosary) seemingly to give the impression of a patriotic Catholic religious crusade. Brigadier-General Mario Benjamin Menéndez was appointed to be the first Governor. A former First Corps commander in northern Argentina, he believed that after seventeen years of largely unfruitful negotiations, occupation was a sufficient political lever for a smooth transition.

Admiral Anaya had spotted that the request by Davidoff presented an opportunity to annex South Georgia; however, Lombardi was anxious the proposal to insert a Project Alpha team would alert the British and he persuaded Anaya to cancel its deployment. Nevertheless, the Junta advanced Operation *Rosario* to no later than 15 May. A British Antarctic Survey field party reported '*Malvinas es Argentina 20 December*' had been scrawled on a wall at Leith.

Davidoff returned to the Embassy on 23 February 1982 and acknowledging he had not completed immigration requirements, mentioned he was hoping to exploit falling scrap prices by completing the contract during the six months of the Southern Hemisphere summer and had appointed a project manager. When the contractors arrived at Leith on 16 March on the *Bahia Buen Suceso*, a British Antarctic Survey party reported that an Argentine flag was being flown ashore and the project manager had yet to complete immigration protocols. Four days later, London informed Buenos Aries the contractors must leave. HMS *Endurance*, the Ice Patrol Ship, departed from Stanley with her Royal Marines Ship's Detachment reinforced by nine NP 8901, giving a total of twenty-two. Ten of her Royal Navy ratings joined NP 8901. When on

22 March, British Antarctic Survey reported that a dozen Argentines were still at Leith and Foreign Secretary Lord Carrington warned Argentine Foreign Minister Costa Mendez that the next day the contractors risked being forcibly removed. Mendez expressed surprise that Great Britain would take such action without exhausting all diplomatic avenues and threatened a strong response. Two days later, Lieutenant Keith Mills RM, who commanded the *Endurance* Ship's Detachment, deployed an observation post to overlook Leith. That night, it reported the naval transport *Bahia Paraiso*, from the Antarctic Squadron, had arrived at Leith. On board was a Project Alpha team commanded by Navy Lieutenant Alfredo Astiz with orders to establish an Argentine presence on South Georgia. In a ceremony, the island was named 'Isla San Pedro' and the national anthem was sung. Astiz had achieved an unenviable reputation at the Navy Petty Officers School of Mechanics interrogation centre and was wanted by France and Sweden for offences against their nationals. The *Bahai Paraiso* sailed next day.

Lombardi was on holiday in Uruguay when he read about the events on South Georgia and immediately returned to Buenos Aries to challenge Anaya. Instead, he was instructed to bring forward Operation *Rosario* and to use any troops and ships that were available and achieve the 'Recovery' before the United Kingdom and the world realised. It is a measure of Lombardi's organisational skills that within the week he had assembled a Task Force. Major-General Osvaldo Jorge Garcia, formerly commander Argentine National Gendarmerie in 1976 and commanding Fifth Corps in Bahia Blanco, was appointed to command the *Malvinas* Theatre of Operations. Under his command was:

- Task Force 20. Support Force. Aircraft-carrier *Veintecinco de Mayo*, naval gunfire and landing craft.
- Task Force 40.1.90. Landing Unit. 2nd Marine Infantry Battalion to capture Port Stanley.
- Task Force 40.2.90, Amphibious Commandos. Capture Moody Brook Barracks and Governor Hunt.
- Task Group 60.1. South Georgia. This group included the Type-69 Class Corvette *Guerrica* with an Embarked Force of 70 marines.

For the first time in a century, Argentine servicemen were being committed to battle. Marine Rear-Admiral Carlos Busser, the deputy to Garcia, addressed his marines:

In the islands we are going to meet a population that we must treat deferentially... They are inhabitants of Argentine territory and, therefore, they have to be treated the same as those who live in Argentina. You will respect personal property and integrity; you will not enter any private residence unless it is necessary for combat reasons. You will respect women, children, elders and men. Be tough to the enemy but also be courteous, respectful and kind to the population of our territory which we have to protect. If anyone engages in rape, robbery, or looting, I will immediately apply the maximum penalty.

On the 28th, the Task Force sailed and hit bad weather, which badly affected the Embarked Force on LST *Cabo San Antonio* of 800 marines.

Between 1806 and 1807, the British attempted to seize Spanish colonies around the River Plate. In first battle in 1806, General William Beresford surrendered in Buenos Aires, a second attacked Montevideo and, after a forty-five-day siege, withdrew with heavy casualties and the third battle, the British withdrew with heavy casualties. Beresford escaped and later commanded Portuguese troops in the Peninsula War in Spain.

*Above left*: General Don Jose de San Martin (1778–1850) played a key role in liberating southern and central South America from Spain. He led an Argentine Army in an alliance that included Great Britain, Portugal and Spain in the Peninsula War. In one battle, he was under Beresford's command.

*Above right*: Argentine officers wearing German Army uniform in the 1920s. The defeat of Germany in the First World War saw increased German immigration to Argentina and former officers importing a Teutonic culture that was still evident in 1982. (Courtesy of Alejandro Amendelora)

Company Ramon Rosa Gimenez of the People's Liberation Army was active in Tucuman Province during the 'Dirty War'. (Courtesy of Alejandro Amendelora)

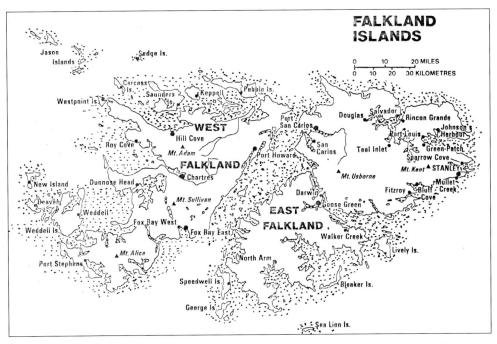

MAP A. Falkland Islands map drawn on board HMS *Fearless* by 3 Commando Brigade illustrators. Maps arrived when the ships were at Ascension.

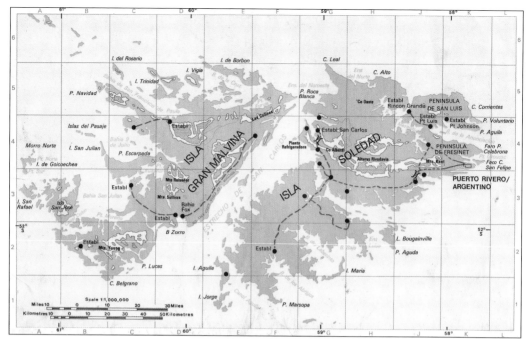

*Above*: MAP B. A map captured at San Carlos showing names in Spanish and the few roads. Helped to reduce misidentification of places.

*Left*: Southern Thule, a British possession, was annexed by Argentina. A 'meteorological' research station was 'protected' by the clandestine Project Alpha team tasked to support Argentine territorial claims in the South Atlantic.

Arctic Patrol Vessel HMS *Endurance* (3,600 tons). With a complement of thirteen officers, 106 ratings and Ship's Detachment of thirteen Royal Marines, she was armed with two 20 mm Oerlikon AA guns and equipped with two Wasp helicopters. Nicknamed 'The Red Plum' from her red hull, she represented British interests in the region and regularly visited Argentine Navy ports.

Port Stanley, 1980.
(Public donation to
3 Commando Brigade
in March 1982)

Stanley. Christ
Church Cathedral,
Ross Road, showing
the whalebone arch.
Consecrated in 1892,
it was the most
southerly Anglican
cathedral and the
parish church of the
Falkland Islands,
South Georgia and
the British Antarctic
Territories.

The Kelper Store,
Stanley.

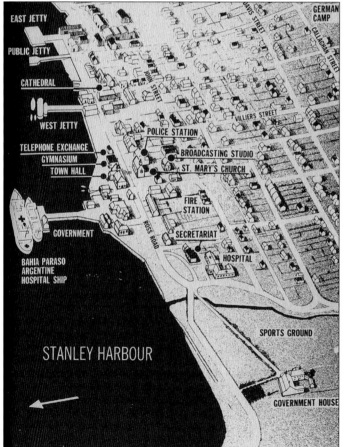

*Above*: A house in Stanley.

*Left*: MAP C. Stanley street plan, 1982. Such maps were used for planning fighting in a built-up town.

# Chapter 2

# Operation *Rosario*: 'Recovery' of Falklands (2 April) and Seizure of South Georgia (3 April)

Harold Briley, the BBC Latin America correspondent, commented in March 1982,

> When you set foot in the Falklands, you feel a sense of isolation. The British Governor and commander-in-chief, who looks after the British Antarctic Territories as well, presides over the largest area left in the British colonies, counting all that expanse of ocean, with just about the smallest population – only 1,800 people, not counting half a million sheep and ten million penguins. There's no television and roads to speak of outside the capital.

When London received intelligence on 31 March that the Argentines intended to invade on 2 April, Prime Minister Thatcher met with her senior Service officers and Secretary of State Defence John Nott and appealed to US President Ronald Reagan to persuade President Galtieri to negotiate, without success.

At 7.30 p.m. on the 1st, Patrick Watts opened the Falkland Island Broadcasting Service (FIBS) regular evening programmes. Forty-five minutes later, Governor Hunt briefed listeners that Argentina was refusing to negotiate over the presence of Argentine nationals on South Georgia without permission and a military threat now existed against the Falklands. The BBC then announced that the UN Security Council had failed to persuade Great Britain and Argentina to settle their dispute. Throughout the night, as Governor Hunt continued to brief. Prime Minister Thatcher was advised on the progress of the Argentine Task Force at 2.45 a.m. on 2 April (10.45 p.m. on 1 April in London) and then at 3.30 a.m., he was advised by the Foreign & Commonwealth Office that:

We have apparently reliable evidence than an Argentine task force will gather off Cape Pembroke early tomorrow morning, 2 April. You will wish to make your dispositions accordingly.

Jack Sollis skippering the government motor coaster *Forrest* on radar watch off Cape Pembroke reported a contact to the east at about 2.45 a.m. This turned out to be the aircraft-carrier *Veintecinco de Mayo*. Hunt briefed the warning from London and during a brief exchange with a caller, insisted he was not going to surrender 'to the bloody Argies'. He declared a State of Emergency and armed himself with his 9 mm Browning, as did his chauffeur, Don Bonner. Chief Secretary Dick Baker and several *Endurance* sailors used the State of Emergency Regulations to intern the LADE staff and about thirty Argentine State Oil Company employees building a new depot in the Town Hall refreshments room. This included Wing-Commander Hector Gilobert, who nearing the end of his posting with LADE. The Canadian Bill Curtis, a former air traffic controller, tried to alter the directional beacon at Stanley Airport but, unable to move it, damaged it with a hammer. King Edward VII Memorial Hospital prepared to receive casualties.

Hunt met with Majors Gareth Noott and Mike Norman at Government House and told them, 'Sounds like the buggers mean it'. The annual rotation of Naval Party 8901 had just been completed with Noott handing over command to Norman at midnight on 1 April. Noott was appointed the Military Advisor to Governor Hunt and controlled the Operations Centre in Government House, and Norman his Tactical HQ on the eastern outskirts of Stanley. His force numbered sixty-nine Royal Marines. Forty-three had just arrived from UK with Norman and was reinforced by Jim Fairfield and Anthony Davies, former Royal Marines, and the ten HMS *Endurance* sailors. The FIDF Armoury provided the additional 7.62 mm FN Self-Loading Rifles. But there were no contingency plans and intelligence appreciations. Unlike the Army defence of Belize focusing on Guatemalan aggression, the Falklands did not receive the same intelligence support from the Royal Navy. In planning likely Argentine strategies, both officers agreed that gently shelving western *Purple* Beach favoured amphibious tracked vehicles and *Orange* Beach at eastern York Bay was suitable for landing craft. Both agreed the Argentines were likely to use landing craft. Naval Party 8901 had little alternative but to conduct a withdrawal in bounds to the citadel of Government House, a solid manse built in 1845. 4 Section, commanded by Corporal Stefan York, positioned at Navy Point and equipped with an 84 mm Carl Gustav recoilless rifles, had orders to engage enemy vessels entering Stanley Harbour and withdraw to pre-dumped supplies in a hide overlooking Port Salvador and provide a point of contact for relief forces.

Twenty-three FIDF and fifteen former reservists who reported to the corrugated Drill Hall in St John's Street were commanded by Major Phil Summers, the Assistant Government Chief Secretary. Several were former Royal Marines who had settled in the Falklands. In the absence of their SLRs, which were sent to NP 8901, most FIDF were equipped with Lee Enfield .303 bolt action rifles. Some converted the Drill Hall into a defensive position and others were deployed to key points such as the Telephone Exchange and the FIBS. Sergeant Gerald Cheek, the Director of Aviation, prepared the Falkland Island Government Air Service Islander for an early morning reconnaissance and deployed a section to disrupt helicopters landing troops landing at the Racecourse. Public Services blocked Stanley Airport runway with trucks.

At about 9.30 p.m. on 1 April, the Argentine Amphibious Commando Group tried to land at Mullet Creek on the south coast using twenty-one motorised inflatables, but long strands of kelp snagging propellers forced them to head west and land at Lake Point. The single Royal Marine on the Sapper Hill observation post reported the outboard engines to Government House. The main body of seventy-six commandos headed the 6 miles for Moody Brooks Barracks but were slowed by the large grass hummocks. Assuming the barracks would be occupied, at 5.30 a.m., the Argentines launched a house clearance tactic using machine-guns and tear gas grenades. It was empty. Most Falklanders were woken by gunfire.

Lieutenant-Commander Pedro Giachino and sixteen commandos tasked to invite Governor Hunt to surrender reached Government House and split into groups covering the east, south and west sides. A year earlier, a visitor claiming to be an architect had been given copies of plans of the building. Alerted by the firing from Moody Brook at 5.30 a.m., Giachino and four commandos broke into Government House and entered the servants' annex. As they approached the main building, the Royal Marines defenders opened fire and wounded Giachino and a lieutenant as they vaulted a wall into the cover of the garden; their three colleagues retreated to the annex. A combat medic sent to treat the two officers was wounded. When Giachino refused to discard a live grenade he was holding, the Royal Marines were reluctant to treat the casualties.

Brian Wells, the Chief Communications Officer, signalled London that the invasion had started and following standard security procedures of wrecking the cipher equipment, locking the Cipher Office and later throwing the keys into the harbour, he was unaware that a technical issue meant his message to the receiving station in Rugby was not received for twenty hours. London was largely unaware of events in Stanley. The HMS *Endurance* naval detachment and secretarial staff destroyed and burnt official and classified documents so efficiently that one Argentine officer later noted there was virtually no intelligence.

At about 4.30 a.m., Tactical Divers landed at Yorke Bay from the submarine ARA *Santa Fe*, recced the beaches and the airport and captured the Cape Pembroke lighthouse. About thirty minutes later, the 2nd Marine Infantry Battalion in LVTP-7s Amtracs landed on *Purple* Beach and were followed by four LARC-5s, each loaded with an Oto Melara 105 mm Pack Howitzer and ammunition, combat stores and medical supplies and a recovery amphibian. A 25th Special Infantry Regiment platoon in a LVTP-7 occupied the airport and raised Argentine flags. Two white anti-submarine warfare Sea King helicopters from the *Almirante Irizar* landed a second marine infantry company and a 105 mm rocket launcher battery. Although a NP 8901 section engaged a LVTP-7, the Argentines quickly reached the eastern outskirts of Stanley and, under orders to limit needless damage and civilian casualties, advanced line abreast through the town. Patrick Watts had placed James Last and his Orchestra on the turntable and was eating a cheese-and-pickle sandwich when six marines entered shouting in Spanish. He discretely activated the microphone so that the commotion could be broadcast, which included him suggesting 'Take the gun out of my back'. At about 7.30 a.m. in the middle of fighting, Chief of Police Ronnie Lamb ordered two police officers to prevent a civilian, Henry Halliday, who was insisting on going to work. The Telephone Exchange was captured and the internees were released from the Town Hall.

By about 8 a.m., the Argentines had control of Stanley and Moody Brook, but Government House was still resisting. When Major Norman suggested to Governor Hunt, sheltering under a large oak table in the Operations Room, that the Royal Marines should break out and establish a 'seat of government' outside Stanley, Hunt agreed surrender was not an option and escaping from Government House seemed unwise. At about 8.35 a.m., Watts patched a message in English to Hunt,

> This is a call to the Colonial British Government on the *Islas Malvinas*. In order to fulfil orders from the Argentine Government, we are here with a numerous task force remaining faithful to our Western and Christian beliefs for the purpose of avoiding bloodshed and property damage to the population. We hope that you will act prudently. Our concern is for the welfare and safety of the people of the *Malvinas*.

When Chief Secretary Baker identified the caller to be a diplomat and former officer who had been instrumental in developing the 'Malvinas' initiative in the 1970s, Hunt asked Watts to stall by asking for the message be repeated. When reports were received that shells were hitting buildings in Stanley, Hunt realised the only sensible option was to seek a ceasefire, but how to contact the Argentines? He telephoned Wing-Commander Gilobert at the LADE, who had just been released from internment in the Town Hall. Gilobert walked up Government House Drive and told several Argentines shooting at him to note he was carrying a white flag. On arriving, he attempted to contact the Argentines using a Royal Marines radio, without success. Meanwhile, Major Norman had instructed Corporal York and 4 Section to 'thin out'. Major Noott and Sergeant Gill were checking the defences and were in the servant's annex when they heard voices from the ceiling. Major Noott fired his Sterling sub-machine gun into the ceiling but his selection lever was on single shot. A burst from Gill convinced three Argentines to surrender. They had taken cover when Giachino vaulted into the garden and were the first Argentine prisoners in the war.

Meanwhile, a flag of truce was fashioned from a white net curtain stretched across an umbrella and Baker and Gilobert walked down Government House Drive and reached the police station on Ross Street. Gilobert then telephoned Patrick Watts and asked him to broadcast a message, in Spanish, asking the 'commander of the forces' to meet a British representative in front of the Catholic church. About twenty minutes later, Marine Vice-Admiral Busser arrived with an escort of six marines and still under occasional shots from Argentines, the parley party returned to Government House. Hunt, who had changed into a pinstriped suit and tie, was waiting in the Governor's office behind his desk, flanked by the two Royal Marines officers. Baker introduced Busser. Hunt responded, 'This is British territory. You are not invited here. We don't want you here. I want you to go, and to take all your men with you now'. Busser retorted that 800 men had landed to recover *Las Malvinas* and he had 2,000 reinforcements. He acknowledged the defence was unexpected and wanted no further fighting. Hunt realised his options were limited and instructed Major Noott to order the defenders to lay down their arms. It was 9.25 a.m.

Arrangements to take Giachino to Stanley Hospital were hindered by the NP 8901 Land Rovers being disabled by gunfire and he died. After the Royal Marines, the Royal Navy and the few FIDF had been disarmed and searched, in an unsavoury gesture, Amphibious Commandos escorted several Royal Marines to Ross Road where they were instructed to lie in front of a LARC-5 amphibian. The order was quickly cancelled. The Royal Marines and FIDF captured in the defence of Government House were assembled on the front lawn. The FIDF was disarmed at the Drill Hall and told to go home.

Major Patricio Dowling then arrived at Government House. A tall and elegant man, he was an experienced counter-intelligence officer detached from the First Corps Intelligence Department in Bahía Blanca and was in command the *Malvinas* Falklands Joint Intelligence Centre and 181 Military Police Company. Of Argentine-Irish parentage, he held strong Irish republican views and was very aware of the long campaign in Northern Ireland against the IRA. He quickly disrespected diplomatic protocol and instructed Hunt to meet Argentine negotiators at the Town Hall. Hunt resisted two hours of bullying until Gilobert suggested he risked arrest.

When General Garcia and Hunt met at 1.15 p.m. at the Town Hall, Hunt refused to shake hands. Garcia said that he was now the Governor of *Las Malvinas*. Hunt replied the invasion was unlawful and ungentlemanly. Nevertheless, terms were formally signed and as the Argentine flag replaced the Union flag at Government House, 149 years of British benign colonial government was replaced by a military regime with a record of ignoring human rights. Chief-Secretary Baker remained for the next three weeks to represent the population. Garcia advised Hunt that he, his family and Royal Marines would be flown out in the afternoon. Hunt was escorted to Government House where he and his wife packed and were then escorted to Baker's house. The Royal Marines were taken in small groups to collect personal belongings from the wreckage at Moody Brook. In the mid-afternoon, Governor Hunt, in his ceremonial uniform, complete with ostrich plumes and sword, and Mrs Hunt were driven to Stanley Airport in the Governor's staff car, a London taxi, by Don Bonner. Major Dowling again breached diplomatic protocol by removing the Governor's pennant from the car and conducted a detailed search of Hunt's luggage. Before he left, Hunt wished the Falkland Islanders good luck and predicted 'The British will be back'. At about 6 p.m., he and his party were flown to Montevideo.

Major-General Garcia announced several recorded communiques in between pre-recorded music:

- No.1. Emphasised the historic Argentina sovereignty over Las Malvinas and welcomed the Falklanders to the nation. He encouraged the population to follow instructions.
- No.2. British civil servants and the military presence to be relieved of their duties and they and their families would be repatriated.
- No.3. The population to remain at home until further notice. Should help be required, a white sheet was to be placed outside the front door. Shops, banks and pubs to be closed.
- No.4. Warning against failing to obey instructions.
- No.5. The population are guaranteed the same rights as in Argentina and continuity of existing way of life, freedom of worship and freedom to enter, leave and remain on the island.

The Falklands Military Committee then issued Communiqué No. 15, to consolidate the Recovery:

1. All measures to be applied by the Malvinas Military Government aims to bring tranquillity to the population, ensure public order, maintain public services and the administration of justice and guarantee the rights of all of its inhabitants.
2. The commitments assumed by the Argentine Republic with the inhabitants of the *Malvinas* during the long period of diplomatic negotiations with Britain will be respected.
3. Efforts will be made to improve the living standards of the population by:
   a. Preserving and increasing the sources of labour as a result of an increase in the commercial interchange.
   b. Improving the facilities of supply from the continent.
   c. Providing new services such as banks, Post Office operating on a permanent basis, television and radio and better medical services. No changes were envisaged on the health and sanitary restrictions on the imports of food and animals.
4. Permanent efforts will be made to respect and preserve the population's way of life.

Patrick Watts was weary and after an emotional broadcast, he closed FIBS. The switchboard informed London that the Falklands was under Argentine occupation.

At about 8.30 a.m. next day, Hunt briefed Prime Minister Thatcher from the British Embassy at Montevideo. At a press conference, he stated surrender was inevitable and the Argentine invasion was reprehensible. The Royal Marines were confined in a swimming pool in an Argentine barracks and repatriated through Uruguay to RAF Brize Norton on 5 April.

## SOUTH GEORGIA, 3 APRIL

About an hour after the Falklands surrender, the Argentine Task Group 60.1 commander, Captain Trombeta, informed Steve Martin, the South Georgia Base Commander, that the Falklands and its dependencies had surrendered and a UN ceasefire was in force; neither were correct. Lieutenant Mills had selected a tussock-covered plateau overlooked by high mountains at King Edward Point as his defensive position and instructed two Royal Marines assault engineers to mine the beaches.

The Argentines attacked at about 11.45 a.m. After the Royal Marines quickly shot down an Army Puma landing troops across King Edward Cove, the *Guerrico* steamed into King Edward Cove to provide support, but even with her 100 mm gun on maximum depression, most shells exploded behind the Royal Marines. She was a large and inviting target and the Royal Marines raked her bridge and decks with heavy fire and as she then went about, Sergeant Peter Leach in Shackleton House added to the chaos by sniping at the bridge. Meanwhile, two Argentine marines delivered by an Alouette to the site of the crashed Puma recovered its light machine-gun and opened fire at the British position. The helicopter and two marines in more flights to the Puma then advanced around King Edward Cove. The *Guerrico*, 3,500 yards out to sea, opened fire on King Edward Point. Lieutenant Mills had planned to evade but his withdrawal to the mountains, lack of support and darkness several hours away limited his options and he signalled his intention by waving a white winter warfare smock. When the Argentines discovered the British numbered twenty-two men, they suspected a ruse.

The Third Junta, December 1981 to June 1982. General Leopoldi Galtieri, Air Force General Basilio Lami Dozo and Admiral Jorge Anaya.

Model of LST *San Antonio*. Four landing craft, 700 Embarked Force, 23 tanks or LVTP-7s, 400 tons of stores. Twelve 40 mm AA guns and a helicopter platform.

Puerto Belgrano. Marines wait to embark on the *Cabo San Antonio*.

*Left*: A chaplain holds a church service on the *Cabo San Antonio* before the landings at Stanley.

*Below*: MAP D. Operation *Rosario*, 2 April 1982. Argentine Landing Plan and NP 8901 defence.

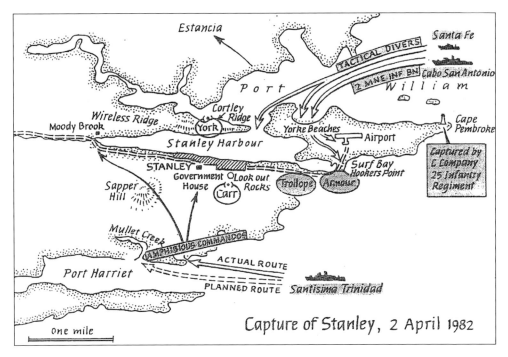

Estancia

Santa Fe

TACTICAL DIVERS

2 MNE INF BN  Cabo San Antonio

P o r t       W i l l i a m

Cortley
Ridge

Wireless Ridge

Moody Brook        York        Yorke Beaches        Cape Pembroke

Stanley Harbour        Airport

STANLEY        Surf Bay        Captured by
Government  Look out        Hookers Point        C Company
House      Rocks   Trollope  Armour        25 Infantry
Sapper        Carr                              Regiment
Hill

Mullet Creek        AMPHIBIOUS COMMANDOS

ACTUAL ROUTE

Port Harriet        PLANNED ROUTE  Santisima Trinidad

**Capture of Stanley, 2 April 1982**

One mile

*Above*: Occupation,
Stanley. View from Ross
Road of the Nurses
Home and Government
House. An Argentine
A-109 Hirundo
helicopter is on the
lawn.

*Right*: Occupation,
Government House.
Combat Aviation
Battalion A-109A
Hirundo helicopter on
the lawn.

2 April. 9 a.m.
Wing-Commander
Gilobert approaches
Government House with
a white flag to parley.

23

NP 8901 are searched by Argentine commandos outside Government House.

Ross Road. NP 8901 prisoners lying on the road in front of a LARC-5 (5-ton Lighter, Amphibious Resupply, Cargo). The photograph caused considerable anger in Great Britain and also breached the Geneva Conventions specifying that prisoners should not be mistreated or humiliated.

Government House. Argentine commandos direct NP 8901 prisoners to Ross Road.

Government House.
Governor Hunt surrenders
to Major-General Garcia. On
his right is Major Patricio
Dowling.

Major-General Garcia and
Marine Vice-Admiral Busser,
the architects of Operation
*Rosario*, leave Government
House. Behind is a Marine
LVTP-7.

Government House. British
prisoners assembled on the
front lawn include Royal
Marines, Royal Navy and
Falkland Island Defence
Force.

Stanley. On the morning of first day of occupation, Falklanders pass a column of LVTP-7s.

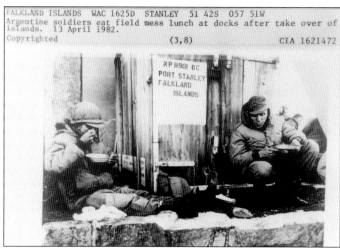

FALKLAND ISLANDS  WAC 1625D  STANLEY  51 42S  057 51W
Argentine soldiers eat field mess lunch at docks after take over of islands.  13 April 1982.
Copyrighted                    (3,8)                    CIA 1621472

Two Argentine marines at Moody Brook Barracks have a meal (Reuters).

A Company, 25th Special Infantry Regiment, captured Stanley Airport. Badge depicts the 'Recovery' of Malvinas.

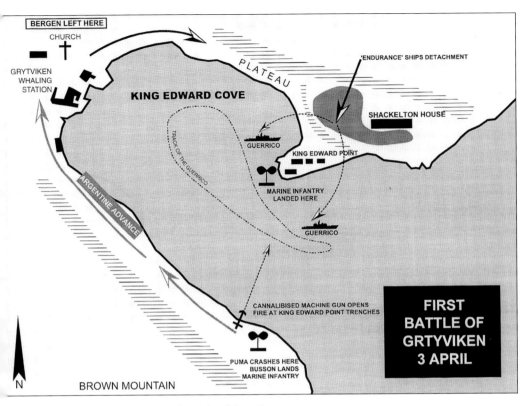

MAP E. South Georgia, 3 April. Battle of Grytviken.

The Argentine Navy A-6 frigate ARA *Guerrica*. 100 mm gun, 40 mm AA gun, two 20 mm and four MM38 Exocets. These were landed in May to provide two land-based launchers.

# Chapter 3

# Occupation of the Falklands

United Nations Security Council Resolution 502 demanded all Argentine forces withdraw and called on Argentina and UK to seek a diplomatic solution, a suggestion that was rejected. Meanwhile, the Argentine Air Force launched Operation *Aries 82* and flew in 9th Infantry Brigade and other troops commanded by Brigadier-General Daher to strengthen the occupation. He had been appointed Chief-of-Staff of the Joint Command of the *Malvinas* Military Garrison.

On 4 April, the naval transport *Isla de los Estados* delivered 9th Engineer Company first to Fox Bay East on West Falkland. It then covered by two Army Puma helicopters landing C Company, 25th Infantry Regiment, commanded by First-Lieutenant Carlos Esteban, at Goose Green. Second-Lieutenant Gomez Centurion spoke reasonably good English. Argentine intelligence listed that the Goose Green Farm Manager, Eric Goss, lived at the Farm Store, however, he had moved to another house ten years previously and the store was now occupied by the storekeeper Keith Bailey. When Bailey offered to take Centurion to see Mr Brook Hardcastle, the Falkland Islands Company Farms General Manager living near Darwin with responsibility for farming across East Falkland, he invited him to ride pillion on his motor bike and careered along the rutted tracks to Brook Hardcastle's house. Centurion used a prepared speech to introduce himself, that Argentina had arrived to liberate the Falklands from colonialism and there were plans to build an air base at Goose Green. Brook Hardcastle was known for his frank views and he told Centurion he preferred that Great Britain protect him. Bailey and Centurion then careered back to Goose Green where Centurion then read the same proclamation to Goss.

Esteban then raised the Argentine flag, celebrated Mass, ordered all civilian weapons and ammunition to be surrendered, changed the Goose Green Post Code and renamed Goose Green and Darwin to be 'Puerto Santiago'. Soldiers conducting a search of Goose Green missed twenty-seven jerrycans of fuel hidden in an early act of resistance. One was left in view. While soldiers searched in house, the husband appeared calm and his wife appeared to be nervous until, without warning, she turned on their record player, opened the windows and turned up the volume for the British National Anthem.

Second-Lieutenant Oscar Reyes, a platoon commander aged twenty-three years, later commented of the Falklanders:

> We treated them as if they were our allies but truly, they never were that. The directives were 'They are Argentineans', but they were not and never will be. They always wanted to make perfectly clear the relation of rejection and reticence. In any case, our exchanges were economic only or limited to trade.

Two days after the occupation of Goose Green, Brook Hardcastle advised Finlay Ferguson, who skippered the Falkland Island Company schooner *Penelope*, that the Stanley Boarding School pupils were being sent home and Ferguson was to ferry those who lived on West Falkland from Egg Harbour, east of Goose Green, to Port Howard where they would be collected by their parents. A couple of days later, the Argentines requisitioned the *Penelope* and dismissed both men. They walked to Goose Green and when they were stopped by a patrol, Finlay's patience snapped and both men were briefly locked up in the Goose Green Community Hall. When a father collected his children from their grandmother in Stanley, the roads were crowded with the Argentine soldiers and military vehicles, his Land Rover clipped an Argentine war correspondent and he was hustled to the Town Hall where he was interned for several hours.

Brigadier-General Mario Menendez arrived as Governor of *Las Malvinas* and Commander-in-Chief on 7 April and moved into Government House. Among his staff was Wing-Commander Carlos Bloomer-Reeve, who was appointed Head of Secretariat. He had posted to the LADE office in Stanley during 1974–75 and had been recalled from the Argentine Embassy in Bonn in late March. Navy Captain Barry Melbourne Hussey had also managed the LADE office and was appointed Secretary of Education, Social Action and Public Health. Both men were fluent in English and had been popular on the Falklands. The Falklands Civil Service remained in post to support the forty-one-strong Civil Affairs Department tasked to:

- Ensure the continuity of education, introduce learning Spanish and teaching Argentine history and geography.
- Facilitate the departure of inhabitants who wished to leave.
- Adjust justice to be in line with legal codes in Argentina.
- Harmonize the Argentine peso as the only legal currency.
- Work with the Argentine Institute of Agricultural Technology to improve pasture and reduce the Falkland Islands Company monopoly.
- Incorporate economic benefits, such as a bank and credit.
- Investigate the exploitation of natural resources and install related industries in order to increase the labour force and stimulate new settlements.
- Maintain the provision of public services such as drinking water, electricity, garbage collection and increase public works.
- Maintain external and internal mail and telecommunication services.

Civil Affairs generally believed the Falkland Islanders to be typical islanders – independent, self-sufficient, distrustful and resourceful. Nicolás Kasanzew, the only Argentine TV reporter in the islands throughout the conflict, identified contempt for

Argentina and that the 'Recovery' equated to 'occupation'. Bloomer-Reeve set out to assure people:

> I wish to categorically assure you that we have not come as conquerors to seize your property or to consider you as our prisoners or vassals. On the contrary, I wish to reaffirm that, as permanently pointed out in our talks maintained since 1967, we are prepared to respect as much as possible the present way of life of the islanders. ... Of course and as from now, we consider you all as inhabitants of the Argentine Republic with the same rights granted by our Constitution and detailed in its Articles 14 such as: to work and exercise any licit industry; to navigate and trade; to make petitions to the authorities; to freely enter, remain, circulate and leave the Argentine territory; to publish their ideas on the press without previous censorship; to use and dispose of your property; to associate for any useful purposes; to freely profess your religion; to reach and learn...

The Government Treasury opened for business and Claims Offices were ordered to pay for chickens or sheep taken by troops, vehicles hired and houses requisitioned.

When the recently arrived Chief of the Falkland Islands Police Force Ronnie Lamb was deported with Governor Hunt, the Falkland Island Police Force resigned, except for Constable Anton Livermore, aged nineteen, and several Special Constables. Livermore had been asked by Chief-Secretary Baker to use his knowledge of fluent Spanish to tread the difficult line between collaboration and loyalty and was assured by Wing-Commander Bloomer-Reeve that it would not jeopardise his loyalty. Livermore became a reassuring presence in his uniform as he helped 181 Military Police maintain law and order. Major Dowling, who regularly carried a British SLR rifle, however regularly used Livermore in internal security and military police tactics used in Argentina of snap identity checks, road blocks, raids on and damage to properties, interrogations and assault. Local representatives responded by negotiating with Civil Affairs that one speculative property search be deemed as sufficient and formal notices 'Searched' be posted on affected properties.

Air photo of part of Goose Green. The long warehouse leading from the jetty is the store. The building topped with a short steeple immediately above is the Community Centre.

*Above left*: 4 April. Marine Rear-Admiral Busser briefs Brigadier-General Menendez, the Governor.

*Above right*: Brigadier-General Menendez in discussion with an officer at Government House. Note nameplate reads 'Governor'.

An Argentine flag flies outside the Falklands Secretariat. This was the centre of the Argentine occupation.

*Left*: The National
Postal and Telegraph
(ECONTEL) provided
postal, telegraphic
and monetary services
from 1972. It was the
equivalent of the British
Post Office.

*Below*: Argentine officers
pose with a Falkland
Islander.

King Edward VII Memorial Hospital in Stanley marked with red crosses.

Two Argentine officers outside the Catholic church in Stanley.

# Chapter 4

# Operation *CORPORATE*

By 1982, the British Armed Forces had been on continuous operations since 1939 and involved in couter-terrorism in Northern Ireland, committed to NATO, particularly in West Germany, and provided garrisons in such places as Belize, Cyprus, Gibraltar and Hong Kong.

After Admiral Sir Henry Leach, the First Sea Lord, had assured Prime Minister Thatcher on 31 March that repossession of the Falklands should not be discounted, Admiral Sir Terence Lewin, the Chief of the Defence Staff, launched Operation *Corporate* to recapture British interests in the South Atlantic. The deployment was the second longest amphibious operation in British military history, the longest being the 8,600 miles launched from Great Britain against Vichy French-controlled Madagascar in 1942. Greenwich Mean Time, in military terms 'Zulu' time, was selected except that UK was on British Summer Time of GMT plus one hour and Argentina was on GMT minus three hours. Most Falkland Islanders resisted by adding the Daylight Summer Time hour, giving a four-hour time difference.

Admiral Sir John Fieldhouse, Commander-in-Chief Fleet, at headquarters at Northwood, and appointed Commander Task Force (CTF), ordered the leading ships to be ready to sail on 5 April. The command structure followed naval principles of the Commander Task Force controlling several Combined Task Groups (CTG) and Task Units (TU). Under command were two aircraft-carriers, HMS *Invincible* and *Hermes*. Rear- Admiral John 'Sandy' Woodward, then on Exercise *Springtrain* at Gibraltar with his 1st Flotilla, was appointed CTG 317.8 on his flagship HMS *Hermes*. Controlling Amphibious Warfare (CTG 317) was Commodore Michael Clapp. Major-General Jeremy Moore, Major-General Royal Marines, was appointed Commander Land Forces with under command 3 Commando Brigade (TU 317.1.1), commanded by Brigadier Julian Thompson, and 5th Infantry Brigade (TU 317.1.2), an Army Home Defence force commanded by Brigadier Tony Wilson. The annual 3 Commando Brigade winter warfare training in Norway had been reduced as a cost-saving measure in 1982, to 42 Commando. It was returning to UK. Moore, Clapp and Thompson were all based in Plymouth, which eased command and control. The two Brigades orders of battle were:

### 3 Commando Brigade

- 40, 42 and 45 Commandos and 2nd and 3rd Battalions, The Parachute Regiment detached from 5th Infantry Brigade.
- 29 Commando Regiment RA celebrating twenty years with the brigade was equipped with three batteries of 105mm Light Guns, giving 18 guns.
- 148 (Meiktila) Commando Forward Observation Battery RA providing naval gunfire support.
- Two Blowpipe sections, Commando Brigade Air Defence Troop.
- T (Shah Shujah's Troop) Battery, 12 Air Defence Regiment providing twelve Rapier firing units.
- 43 Air Defence Battery, 32nd Guided Weapon Regiment.
- Mountain and Arctic Warfare Cadre.
- Special Boat Service (SBS).
- Two Troops of the Blues and Royals with Scimitar and Scorpions tracked reconnaissance vehicles
- Special Air Service, 22 SAS.

### 5th Infantry Brigade

- 2nd Scots Guards, 1st Welsh Guards and 1/2nd Gurkha Rifles.
- Two batteries of 4th Field Regiment giving twelve guns. The third battery had just returned from six months in Belize.

Both brigades had integral signals, logistic, air defence, engineer, medical and intelligence support. Argentine tactics and the need for visual acquisition forced Navy and Army gunners to adopt firing at the rear of the aircraft, as opposed to the front or side. Prior to deployment, 5th Brigade spent a 'shake down' fortnight training in Wales, however one week was unseasonably hot. Crucial was the Royal Fleet Auxiliary (RFA) fleet of tankers, roll-on/roll-off logistic and general support ships and 'Ships Taken Up From Trade' hired by the Ministry of Defence including troopships, tugs and vessels converted to hospital ships. A constant flow of tankers visiting friendly West African ports kept the ships supplied with fuel.

Commanders, at all levels, have responsibility for intelligence supplied. Fundamental to solving the problem is the never-ending Intelligence Cycle of collecting, collating, evaluation, converting and producing the product in time to be of use. The Army had Intelligence Corps had intelligence and security sections supporting the Ministry down to brigades. Battalions and regiments formed sections commanded by an intelligence officer. Commanders rejecting intelligence is not unknown. In spite of the historical threat, the Ministry of Defence failed to predict the Argentine 'Recovery'. Argentina had, for instance, purchased its map requirement from a military map depot.

Operational Intelligence sets out to predict enemy activities. Human Intelligence exploits prisoners of war, refugees, local civilians, informants and gossip. An Interrogation resource was formed from linguists in the Task Force. A debriefing organisation interviewed people repatriated to UK. Naval Party 8901 was not debriefed on returning to UK; fortunately, Major Norman wrote a comprehensive report. In relation to Signals Intelligence, the Ministry of Defence also liaised with amateur radio enthusiasts. Document Exploitation examines documents, manuals, maps and postal intercept. The Intelligence Corps provided Protective Security and Counter-intelligence advice against espionage, sabotage, subversion and terrorism. Admiral Anaya instructed his Naval Intelligence to examine raiding the British naval bases at Portsmouth and Plymouth, but they were found to be guarded against Irish terrorism. Operation *Algeciras*, an attack in Gibraltar, was undermined by the Spanish Police. When the Argentine freighter *Rio de la Plata* was sighted several miles west of Ascension on 24 April, the crew of a helicopter scrambled to intercept and took photographs of several long tubes on her decks thought to be human torpedoes; they were not. A suspected infiltration three days later led to Royal Marines sweeping the island. While nothing of interest was found, counter-sabotage measures included patrolling warships, boat crews of ships at anchor dropping grenades and ships leaving the anchorage at night. Fortunately, good weather favoured the British. A Joint Service Imagery detachment on the two aircraft carriers supported air operations. Photographs taken by Terry Peck, the former Chief of Police, using a camera fitted with a telephoto lens inserted into a drainpipe, was smuggled to UK by a civilian. The public donated photographs.

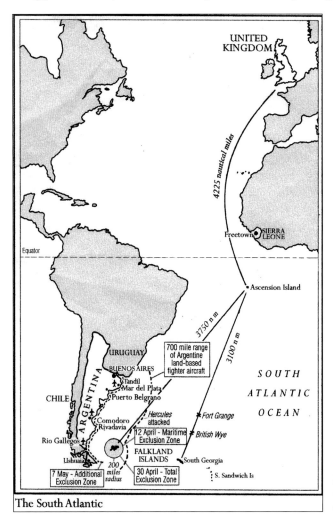

MAP F. Operation *CORPORATE*'s Area of Operational Deployment.

Ascension Island, a sleepy and isolated British Territory with 360 degrees observation of an approach, Wideawake Airfield with a long runway and also with decent anchorage, was the logical forward operating base. Great Britain escalated the crisis a week after the 'Recovery' by announcing a 200-miles Maritime Exclusion Zone around the Falklands and warned Argentina that from 12 April, her warships 'trespassing' on British interests would be 'treated as hostile'. A nuclear submarine lurking in the region was implied. Great Britain also warned that 'all Argentine vessels, including merchant vessels or fishing vessels apparently engaged in surveillance and intelligence gathering against British forces in the South Atlantic would also be regarded as hostile.' Argentina responded next day by establishing a 200-miles defence zone along its vulnerable Atlantic coast and absorbed the Falklands Theatre of Operations into the South Atlantic Theatre of Operations Command.

HMS *Hermes*, the Operation Corporate Flagship. Launched in 1953, and weighing 23,000 tons, she carried fifteen Sea Harriers, six RAF Harriers, six Sea King HAS-5s anti-submarine, two Lynx and a Wessex-5. (Crown Copyright)

HMS *Intrepid*. One of two Landing Platform Dock Amphibious Assault Ships (11,000 tons standard). Four Landing Craft (Utility) and four Landing Craft (Vehicles and Utility). Embarked Force of 650 troops, six 105 mm guns and four assault helicopters. Her sister ship was HMS *Fearless*, which controlled amphibious operations. (Crown Copyright)

HMS *Fearless* Amphibious Operations Room at Action Stations viewed from the Intelligence Desk. A member of the 3 Commando Brigade Intelligence Section plots on the battle map.

Early intelligence. A photo of east Stanley showing Moody Brook. The image was sourced from the Radio and Space Research Laboratory Station, Slough.

Early intelligence. One of several photos taken by former Falklands Chief of Police Terry Peck, smuggled to the UK by a teacher and delivered to 3 Commando Brigade Intelligence Section at sea. Probable marine infantry air defence position near Stanley. (Terry Peck)

A Wessex prepares to lift a consignment from the HMS *Fearless* Flight Deck. On the deck are 29 Commando Regiment 105 mm Light Guns and HQ 3 Commando Brigade Swedish Bandvagn 202 (BV 202) tracked articulated, all-terrain vehicles, some carrying skis. (Author)

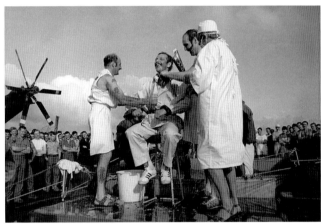

HMS *Fearless* crossing the line. A centuries-old rite of passage celebrating Father Neptune and his royal court coercing the 'pollywogs' (tadpoles) into 'the Ancient Order of the Deep'. In this instance, the author is crossing for the third time. (Crown Copyright)

Ascension. Georgetown on the west coast is the capital of the British Overseas Territory of Saint Helena, Ascension and Tristan da Cunha. Named after King George III, the island was first garrisoned by the Admiralty in 1815. (Author)

*Above*: A view of Ascension Island from Green Mountain to the Task Force anchorage. Two boats village in the centre. (Author).

*Left*: Ascension. Weapon training. A 40 Commando 81 mm mortar team on live firing adopt the 'mortar stoop' as the weapon is fired. (Crown Copyright)

Ascension. A FV 107 76 mm Scimitar of B Squadron, Blues and Royals. (Crown Copyright)

*Above*: Ascension. A Sea King delivers a consignment as part of the logistic programme to ensure the right equipment was in the correct place for landings. Helicopters were crucial. (Crown Copyright)

*Right*: Ascension. HMS *Fearless* 40 mm Oerlikon gun crew live firing. Some of the audience gave points for accuracy and style. (Author)

# Chapter 5

# The Argentine Defence and Falklands Occupation

The Argentine journalist Haroldo Foulkes visiting the Falklands was shocked to discover that the territory that he understood to be Argentine was British in culture, language and customs. Journalists were disappointed not to be met by a repressed Spanish-speaking population and Argentine servicemen were confused by the absence of cheering crowds in Stanley waving blue and white flags and no encouragement to fraternise with the population. An educated conscript was more realistic, 'It was an intellectual contradiction to think that we were in our land. Truly, it looked more as if we were invading an English coastal village.'

The British reaction to the 'Recovery' and possibility of hostilities led to Argentina deploying the 10th Mechanised Infantry Brigade commanded by Brigadier-General Oscar Luis to 'Las Malvinas'. It was built around 3rd, 6th and 7th Infantry Regiments.

The Argentine Army was a major backbone of the nation. It had contributed to Chilean and Peruvian independence and had pacified the indigenous populations but for the last fifty years, senior generals, admirals and airmen had been involved in political power-broking, which undermined national stability. Combined operations tended to be dysfunctional. In common with other South and Central American armed forces, the social, cultural and philosophical differences between the Army officer, the regular and the conscript was distinct.

In 1982, the Army was divided into five corps of twelve brigades of two Armoured Cavalry, two Mountain, two Airborne and the remainder Mechanised Infantry. Regimental spirit of formations, units and bases were built around a military personality; for instance the 3rd 'General Manuel Belgrano' Infantry Regiment commemorated the early eighteenth-century soldier and intellectual who chose the blue and white national colours when he led the Argentine liberation from Spain in 1801. The average Argentine infantry regiment numbered about 700 men against 650 of a British battalion. Organisation was similar with three rifle companies each of three platoons, a headquarters and command company, a support company of recce and anti-tank platoons and a logistics company providing supplies and medical support. A difference was that first-lieutenants commanded companies whereas the British Army appointed majors and the Royal Marines selected captains. Padres were key components. When reservists were mobilised in 1982, several fifth-year cadets were quickly commissioned as platoon commanders. Combat and service support in brigades were identified by the number of the brigade, thus 10th Logistic Battalion supported 10th Brigade.

Officers usually joined a brotherhood, such as founded by General San Martin in the 1800s, to promote the concept of the Army as defender of the nation, guardian of tradition and pillar of society. Cadets graduated through the National Army Academy, which was modelled on the US West Point. Captains and majors attended a middle management staff college course and had opportunities to take a degree and attend foreign staff colleges and courses. Potential generals attended the joint service National War College.

Career NCOs were generally Regulars. An aide memoire entitled *Orientation Manual for the Recently Graduated NCO* (1981) included chapters on the nation, sanctity of marriage and family and introduction to capitalism, communism, socialism and liberalism. Other chapters related to military communications, tactics, weapons at regimental, company and platoon level, vehicle maintenance and military report writing. Conscription was regarded as crucial to the cultural, spiritual, political and national way of life of Argentina. Introduced into the Army in 1901, conscripts remained at the bottom of the pecking order. Field punishment and punches were common. There was little bonding of the shared experiences that solidified relationships between British Regulars. By 1976, the one-year conscription beginning in January consisted of nine months basic training and specialist training such as medics and clerks and the last three months were either on operations or '*colimba*', the nickname derived from the words '*corra*' ('run'), '*limfoot*' ('clean') and '*barra*' ('sweep'), referring to main occupations of the soldiers. The British equivalent was 'fatigues'. Conscripts could be promoted to *Dragoneante*, which equates roughly to the US Army Private First Class. On discharge, soldiers were usually transferred to the National Guard Reserve and then to the home defence Territorial Guard.

The Marine Corps and Navy drafted conscripts in bi-monthly successive rotations over fourteen months service, which meant that there was always a cadre of experience. Within four days of receiving orders on 8 April to deploy, a 700-strong Marine battlegroup built around the 5th Marine Infantry Battalion, supported by field and air defence artillery, engineers and logistics, occupied a 12-mile perimeter around Mount Tumbledown, Mount William and Sapper Hill, west of Stanley. The Marines used naval ranks and terminology and were a product of superior training and the institutionalised leadership. The battalion was based in Tierra del Fuego in Patagonia and was familiar with the rigorous climate of the approaching winter.

3rd Artillery and 4th Airborne Artillery Groups with three four-gun batteries and a Marine battery an artillery group of thirty airportable Oto Melara M56 105 mm Pack Howitzers. In the last week of the war, a four-gun 155 mm battery arrived. The Royal Artillery batteries of six guns had recently exchanged their Pack Howitzers for 105 mm Light Guns. There was a significant air defence capability. The Engineer Group *Malvinas* was formed from 9th and 10th Engineer Companies. 601 Engineer Group and

Amphibious Engineers laid an estimated 25,000 mines in 119 minefields covering a total of 12 square miles. The sappers also performed credibly as infantry

A National Frontier Force was formed to defend the new border on *Las Malvinas* and control internal security. The Force included 601 and 602 Army Commandos, usually consisting of a headquarters and three sixteen-man assault sections, each commanded by a captain and a support section and were identifiable by a dark green beret. After training, men were either posted to a commando unit or returned to their parent arm to await recall for Special Forces duty, a system that introduced inherent weaknesses in developing expertise and team spirit. The 7th Counter-Insurgency Helicopter Squadron supported the Air Force Special Operations Group with air despatch, heavy drop and search and rescue and the Combat Control Team provided pathfinders for the 4th Airborne Brigade. Both had rapid unloading and loading of aircraft skills. Other elements of the National Border Force included the Coastguard, Border Guards and national police.

Argentine logistics was severely criticised during the 1978 Beagle Channel crisis with Chile. The Naval Transport Service used its fleet and requisitioned Falklands Islands Company coasters to support the garrisons outside Stanley; however, enemy action and poor distribution often meant that conscripts adapted, for instance by slaughtering sheep. The Argentine medical system lacked basic supplies. Part of King Edward VII Hospital was used as a military hospital. Insufficient ambulances in Stanley meant casualty evacuation was weak.

Faith was important. Some younger priests were distributors of religious-political pamphlets. Father Torrens was teaching at a Comodoro Rivadavia school when he deployed on 2 April and was expected to conduct eight masses a day. One night in mid-June, he was with a Pack Howitzer battery that was forced by naval gunfire to move in heavy rain. The priority next morning was Mass.

For the majority of the Falklanders, negotiation with a country whose territorial claim was tenuous and who owned an unenviable human rights and democracy record was out of the question. In his first meeting with influential members of the community, Menéndez insisted he had no desire to disrupt the way of life and suggested that if there was resistance, the Falklands Islands Company would be involved. Richard Stevens, a teacher who had moved from Kent in the late 1970s and lived near Estancia, had several conversations with First-Lieutenant Ignacio Gorriti, who commanded the Air Mobile Reserve (Combat Team *Solari*) on Mount Kent, and rejected his suggestion that Argentina would improve the quality of life, such as build roads. Stevens replied that if he wanted to live in a place with roads, he would, however he liked his country and 'wanted to be left alone'.

Aware of the danger of clandestine radio from their 'Dirty War' experiences, an Argentine intercept company arrived on 2 April to monitor civilian internal and external transmissions. Civil Affairs instructed those living in Stanley were instructed to surrender transceivers to the military authorities at the Town Hall and those living in the 'camp' were to decommission their sets and bury the valves. However, doctors at King Edward VII Memorial Hospital warned that removing radios in the 'camp' could lead to fatalities and extracted an agreement that radios at Hill Cove, Goose Green and Darwin be retained. Fox Bay East had concealed an illicit radio by dispersing parts in dead letter boxes.

When the journalist Larry Margolis returned to the BBC on 2 April after an overseas posting, he found the only report was a cable and wireless Falklands station suggesting 'we have a lot of new friends'. The BBC amateur radio club was in the Langham Hotel, formerly a BBC office block, and a manager encouraged him to use his amateur radio expertise to trawl the airwaves. During the afternoon, he contacted Bob McLeod at Goose Green. It was he who reported the Argentine flag was flying over Government House.

While the BBC had struggled for information, the Ministry of Defence was having success. Les Hamilton, formerly of the Royal Signals and a printer living in Clydebank, had been an enthusiast since a teenager. Among his global network was Tony Pole-Evans, a sheep farmer on Saunders Island, 80 miles north-west of Stanley and the site of Port Egmont of the British landing in 1765. Shortly before the Argentine invasion, Hamilton and Pole-Evans had agreed a security identification code known only to the two men indicating radio frequencies to be used. They agreed to communicate in short burst transmissions at 4.20 p.m. GMT daily. When Hamilton learnt of the Argentine invasion, he relayed information from Pole-Evans to the Ministry of Defence and Downing Street. Conscious that his 45-foot mast would attract attention, Pole-Evans used a more compact antenna. Hamilton used his knowledge of military map marking to plot information onto a large map in his house that was regularly reviewed by a military intelligence officer, who warned him that if Pole-Evans was caught, he would doubtless be shot. Hamilton tasked Pole-Evans to collect specific information, such as locations, exercises, minefields and the results of naval gunfire and bombing. Hamilton's wife, Pilar, a Spanish lecturer at Strathclyde University, translated anything in Spanish. The information was sent to Defence Intelligence and despatched as Intelligence Summaries (Int Sum) and Reports (Int Reps) to the Task Force, each report graded for accuracy and classification. Some information graded as 'Immediate' sometimes reached Task Force intelligence officers within minutes of being reported by Hamilton. Towards the end of the war, Pole-Evans hosted a SBS patrol for three weeks.

Bob North, a North Yorkshire debt controller, was in contact with Reginald Silvey, the Cape Pembroke assistant lighthouse keeper living in Stanley, made redundant when the Argentines extinguished the lamp. Silvey was a keen radio enthusiast who had camouflaged his antenna in his kitchen as a washing line. He had also acquired a 'Searched' notices. He mentioned aircraft were using Stanley Airport to fly in supplies and ammunition and since there were no islanders in the area, it could be safely attacked. He also used military abbreviations, such as 'AA' (anti-aircraft) and 'APC' (armoured personnel carrier) and when this confused North, Silvey suggested such information be transmitted verbatim to the Ministry of Defence. North arranged for one urgent intelligence report to be collected by the Bridlington Police and taken by motorcyclist to the Ministry of Defence.

The Argentines were convinced that information was being transmitted from the area of the West Store in Stanley and conducted several raids and electronic sweeps without success. Eileen Vidal, the senior Switchboard radio/telephone operator married to a Chilean, managed the Government Radio-Telephone (RT) network. Fluent in Spanish, she defied Argentine instructions that civilians were not to contact ships by passing intelligence. When HMS *Endeavour* was within range, she began with 'I'm not surprised to be talking to you, but ...', a preamble that became a defiant catchphrase in the town.

When Northwood instructed HMS *Endurance* to meet the Task Force, this left a gap in the intelligence collection. The interception of conversations between Stanley Boarding School pupils and parents provided useful intelligence of Argentine activity. While the 2-metre Citizens Band (CB) network lacked the privacy of a telephone, in the absence of newspapers, it enhanced community spirit particularly during air raids. Doctor's Hour was a crucial community resource.

The authorities used the FIBS studio to introduce LRA60 *Radio Islas Malvinas,* as part of a regional network promoting national and local news, culture and history. It was managed by Norman Powell, an Anglo-Argentina radio announcer. Even though the equipment was failing, Islanders still supported Patrick Watts. The BBC World Service and the twice weekly BBC Overseas Service *London Calling the Falklands* provided news, light entertainment and morale-boosting messages between relatives and friends. Peter King, a retired BBC announcer, always ended his programmes with 'Heads down, Hearts high'. Increasing success in jamming transmissions were undermined by two war correspondents who landed at San Carlos and alerted the BBC. The Ministry of Defence spokesman Ian MacDonald gave daily briefings using maps and pointers and reassured listeners with his restrained delivery and, to the delight of listeners, frustrated self-important journalists by supplying mysterious answers to their questions.

The Falklands did not have television and when Argentine technicians built a studio in the former FIBS and offered 100 colour and black-and-white televisions donated by the Province of Misiones in north-eastern Argentina for purchase or hire LU78, Channel 7 transmitted its first two-hour television evening broadcast introduced by Norman Powell on 13 April in Spanish and English. The scheme was greeted with some derision by a population weaned on the BBC World Service and scornful of propaganda, particularly originating from Argentina.

The nature of the occupation led to active resistance being necessarily low-key. Tension increased in the first week when 4 Section arrived the house of Long Island Farm owned by Neil and Glenda Watson. His family had arrived in the Falklands in 1840. Watson informed Wing-Commander Gilobert, who suggested the Royal Marines remain with him, but Major Dowling heard about them and arrived with soldiers in three Pumas protected by two Pucara flying top cover. Soldiers roughed up the Royal Marines, tied them and flew to Stanley where they were interned in the police station until repatriated.

Councillor William Luxton could trace his heritage in Chartres on East Falkland to the mid-1840s. The day before the invasion, he and his wife flew to Stanley during the crisis. Intending to fly back next day, he went to the Town Hall for his route and to identify his aircraft. Dowling refused his request and told him that since he was of security interest, he should not cause trouble. When Luxton and his wife returned to Chartres by road and a boat, Dowling was furious and raided the farm with a squad of military police and beat up several civilians. He then arrested Luxton and his family at Chartres and confined them to Government House, along with Chief Secretary Baker and his wife and Chief Secretary Ray Checkley. Three days later, they and eight others were deported to Montevideo and flown to UK where they were debriefed. Luxton gave numerous interviews to the media about his experiences.

Resistance was difficult and necessarily low. Public Works Department (PWD) employees in Stanley maintaining water and electricity services resisted by drawing the line at any project benefitting the occupation. Ron Buckett, a former soldier who managed the Plant and Transport Authority, confined sabotage to 'explainable' faults to equipment hired by the Argentines. When teachers objecting to the Argentine curriculum were replaced by Argentine Ministry of Education teachers, they were also debriefed on returning to the UK. PWD posters urging Argentine troops to keep Stanley clean by using waste bins and marked with 'Malima' (*Mantenga Limpia Malvinas* – 'Keep *Malvinas* Clean') were defaced with a Falklander dressed in a woolly hat and wellington boots kicking an Argentine soldier towards a Royal Marine who drop-kicked him into a bin. No sooner were they removed, more would appear. A nurse smuggled a Union Jack into King Edward VII Memorial Hospital and unfurled it at the birth of Sian Davies, one of three 'war babies' born under the flag during the occupation. When the Secretariat flagpole snapped in high winds, a vociferous lady informed the occupants that the Argentina flag lying on the ground was a sure sign their presence was limited. Philip Middleton, a British Government official who had refused evacuation, and Steve Whitley, the vet, secured the properties and contents of civil servants repatriated to UK and took photographs of abandoned property being used as billets and defensive positions. When properties were requisitioned, Whitley cut 'phone lines with gelding scissors'. FIDF Sergeant Cheek snipped military telephone cables.

After about three weeks, Constable Livermore insisted that the demands of Major Dowling had become intolerable and he asked Terry Peck if the matter could be referred to Monsignor Daniel Spraggon, an Englishman and the Papal Representative of the Falkland Islands and South Georgia. He usually wore his formal regalia and regularly intervened on behalf of the Falklanders. Unfortunately, Dowling had found police files buried by Peck and was using the information. Peck was formerly on the Legislative Council and a vigorous opponent of transfer of sovereignty and when Sir Nicholas Ridley, Minister of State at the Foreign & Commonwealth Office, had visited in 1980 to promote leasing the Falklands, he fitted his Land Rover with a loudhailer and invited protestors to barrack the minister as he was being driven to the airport. Wing-Commander Bloomer-Reeve was sympathetic to Livermore's request and accepted his resignation. When Livermore warned Peck that Major Dowling planned to arrest him, Peck immediately left Stanley on a borrowed motorbike and arrived at Long Island Farm, where Neil and Glenda Watsons were hosting the Queen's birthday. Unfortunately, no one heard the Puma helicopter delivering a cordon-and-search party and two Pucara flying top cover. Nevertheless Peck successfully hid in a toilet. Next day, he collected cold weather clothing and rations left by sailors from HMS *Endurance* and for the next ten days evaded capture in the remote Geordie's Valley until approaching winter persuaded him to seek shelter from the Morrisons at Brookfield Farm.

By mid-April, the Falklands Military Garrison strategy was to deny a British landing manoeuvre room by using Mountain and Commando reinforcements. There were several VIP visits. General Christino Nicolaides, commanding First Corps, said he 'would be with the troops' and mentioned they had twenty days to build a 'fortress'. It was his only visit. The following day, Menendez escorted President Galtieri on a wide-ranging itinerary by helicopter and held discussions at Moody Brook, but he did not meet any field commanders. On 24 April, 601 Commando Company arrived. Formed in January in 1982 as Team Hawk 8 for the 1978 World Cup by Lieutenant-Colonel Mohamed Alí Seineldín, who was now commanding 25th Special infantry Regiment, the Commando spent its first night at Moody Brook and then Major Dowling used it for road blocks and intensified patrols.

In the mid-afternoon, fourteen Falklanders identified as 'troublemakers' were given thirty minutes to pack. Included was Velma Malcolm, the chair of the hostile Falkland Islands Association and part-owner of the Rose Hotel. Sergeant Cheek was one of four FIDF known for their marksmanship. A few days earlier, he had been summoned to the police station and in a frank exchange of views with Major Dowling, was warned if he caused trouble, he could find himself 'in a very serious situation'. His family was instructed to pack, but he convinced the Argentines his elderly parents and his family should remain in Stanley. The fourteen were told since their destination was 'internal', they did not need their passports and were then escorted to a C-130 Hercules loading some soldiers. Fearing visions of being dumped into the 'Atlantic', the group was flown by helicopter to Fox Bay West for the night and then taken to Fox Bay East next morning. The lieutenant commanding an engineer platoon at the farm admitted he had no idea why the group had been sent and arranged for Farm Manager Richard Cockwell to find billets. While there was generally enough food, drinking water was short until Cockwell excavated a well in the garden. The deportations had profound impact in Stanley because the arrests had been sudden; no one knew where the fourteen were until information leaked that they had been exiled to 'an internment camp'. Bloomer-Reeve clarified this to be in a 'rural' zone on the Falklands. Monsignor Spraggon warned Governor Menendez not to treat the Falklands as a dictatorship.

The 'Air Bridge', April 1982. Argentine troops carrying bulky US-style kitbags arriving at Military Air Base Stanley pass an Argentine Air Force C-130 Hercules. The 'Air Bridge' between Stanley and Argentine bases flew 421 missions in April. The number fell to thirty-one between 1 May and 14 June, which had a major impact on supplying stores and ammunition.

5 April. One of several clandestine photos taken by former Director of Aviation Gerald Cheek of a Navy Electra transport aircraft flying troops to Military Air Base Stanley. Cheek was also FIDF. (Gerald Cheek)

Stanley. Argentine soldiers pass along Ross Road towards defensive positions west of Stanley.

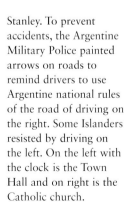

Stanley. To prevent accidents, the Argentine Military Police painted arrows on roads to remind drivers to use Argentine national rules of the road of driving on the right. Some Islanders resisted by driving on the left. On the left with the clock is the Town Hall and on right is the Catholic church.

The Air Force 2nd Early Warning Group controlled Army and Air Force air defence. Rh-202 gunners on Stanley Common. The Rheinmetall Mk 20 RH-202 is a 20 mm cannon for air and ground defence.

Stanley Common. An Argentine 81 mm mortar team.

A Panhard AML 245 armoured car. Used by 10 Armoured Recce Squadron, the AML was crewed by the commander, radio operator and the driver. It was fitted with a 90 mm quick-firing gun and night vision devices. 181 Squadron also deployed but was dismounted.

*Above left*: Two Argentine sappers. Minefield signage disappeared in the wind and maps were lost when positions were overrun. An estimated 4,000 anti-vehicle and 20,000 anti-personnel mines were laid.

*Above right*: British cartoon commenting on Argentine minelaying.

Four conscripts, two with garden spades, outside a bunker. Army conscripts served one year of national service.

Stanley Common. A padre flanked by two officers in front of a lorry being used as a bunker. The padre had wound plastic bags around his knees.

An Army captain, two sergeants-majors (sitting left) and four soldiers at a bunker on Stanley Common.

Two Argentine conscripts washing clothes in a small wash basin. Behind them is their bunker.

An Argentine field
cookhouse brought
onto a tactical position.
Those at the end usually
received lukewarm food,
if any at all.

An Argentine field
cookhouse.

Conscripts enjoying a
meal.

DGOS FORM 494
(Revised 1984)

## MENU SHEET AND COOKING INSTRUCTIONS

## 24-HOUR RATION GS

The content of each pack differ and a different pack should be issued each day.

| MENU 'A' | MENU 'B' | MENU 'C' | MENU 'D' |
|---|---|---|---|
| **BREAKFAST** | **BREAKFAST** | **BREAKFAST** | **BREAKFAST** |
| Porridge | Porridge | Porridge | Porridge |
| Bacon Grill | Baconburger | Bacon Grill | Baconburger |
| Biscuits Brown | Biscuits Brown | Biscuits Brown | Biscuits Brown |
| Chocolate Drink | Chocolate Drink | Chocolate Drink | Chocolate Drink |
| **SNACK** | **SNACK** | **SNACK** | **SNACK** |
| Biscuits Brown | Biscuits Brown | Biscuits Brown | Biscuits Brown |
| Ham Spread | Beef Spread | Chicken Spread | Chicken & Bacon Spread |
| Chocolate Full Cream | Chocolate Full Cream | Chocolate Full Cream | Chocolate Full Cream |
| Spangles | Boiled Sweets | Confectionery Bar | Spangles |
| Chocolate Covered Caramel | Chocolate Covered Caramel | Chocolate Covered Caramel | Chocolate Covered Caramel |
| Dextrose Tablets (Lemon) | Dextrose Tablets (Orange) | Dextrose Tablets (Lemon) | Dextrose Tablets (Orange) |
| **MAIN MEAL** | **MAIN MEAL** | **MAIN MEAL** | **MAIN MEAL** |
| Biscuit Fruit Filled | Biscuit Fruit Filled | Biscuit Fruit Filled | Biscuit Fruit Filled |
| Instant Soup | Instant Soup | Instant Soup | Instant Soup |
| Chicken Curry | Steak & Kidney Pudding | Steak & Onion Casserole | Minced Steak |
| Pre-cooked Rice | Spaghetti in Tomato Sauce | Beans in Tomato Sauce | Mixed Vegetables |
| Apple Flakes | Apple & Apricot Flakes | Fruit Salad | Mixed Fruit Pudding |

**DRINKS**
Instant Skimmed Milk, Sugar, Tea, Coffee, Beef Stock Drink and Orange/Lemon Powder.

**SUNDRIES**
Chewing Gum, Toilet Paper, Salt, Book Matches, Waterproof Matches, Can Opener, Water Purification Tablets and Menu Sheet.

**Note:** Contents may vary from printed menu sheets, depending on items available at time of packing.

*Above*: The reality is that the British blockade interrupted the regular delivery of supplies and troops outside Stanley, who supplemented the rations by slaughtering sheep, without and with permission. The Falklanders were also rationed.

*Left*: British individual twenty-four-hour ration menu, usually known as 'Compo' (Composite).

24 April, Stanley Airport. 25th Infantry Regiment parade to swear the Oath of Allegiance to the Argentine flag. Father Torrens, a military padre, in cassock; Brigadier-General Daher (Chief-of-Staff); Lieutenant-Colonel Seineldin (Commanding Officer) with sword; and Major Carlos María Vergara (Second-in-Command).

The 25th Infantry Regiment took a statue of Our Lady of Luján, a sixteenth-century icon of the Virgin Mary usually displayed in the Basilica of Luján, to the Falklands and lodged it in the Catholic church in Stanley. It was captured and transferred to the Catholic Church of St Michael and St George in Aldershot to commemorate the 255 British, 649 Argentine servicemen and three civilians who died in the war. In October 2019, after a joint audience with Pope Francis, a British military chaplain returned Our Lady to an Argentine chaplain. A replica was sent to Aldershot.

22 April.
Brigadier-General
Menendez in discussion
with President Galtieri
during his only visit to the
Falklands.

Moody Brook. Officers
in discussion with
Galtieri (unseen at the
table) are (left to right)
Brigadier-General Néstor
Castelli (Commander
Engineers); Monseñor
Victorio Bonamín (Military
Proctor), who created a
military vicariate 'to attend
the spiritual care of the
military of the land, sea
and air'; Brigadier-General
Jofre (Commander
10th Brigade); and
Brigadier-General
Menéndez.

From left to right:
Brigadier-General José
Julio Mazzeo (Deputy
Commander, 2nd Army
Corps) with cap and
gloves; Lieutenant-Colonel
Seineldín (CO 25th
Infantry Regiment in
beret); and Colonel Juan
Ramón Mabragaña (CO
5th Infantry Regiment)
before joining his regiment
at Port Howard. In the
background is a C-130.

# Chapter 6

# Approach to Battle

Argentina was showing little sign of abandoning her ambitions. Northwood assessed that the recapture of South Georgia would demonstrate British resolve, but failure would present Argentina with an opportunity to humiliate Great Britain.

Shortly before 3 Commando Brigade deployed in the second week of April, Major-General Moore instructed Brigadier Thompson to supply a company for a sensitive mission. He chose M Company, 42 Commando, which had just spent three months on the annual winter deployment in Norway.

On 7 April, Captain Brian Young, the commanding officer of the guided missile destroyer HMS *Antrim*, was appointed to command CTG 317.9 and instructed in Operation *Paraquet* to recapture South Georgia. Under his command as Commander Land Forces was Major Guy Sheridan, a highly experienced winter warfare and mountain leader and 42 Commando second-in-command. Other units included the destroyer HMS *Plymouth*, the Fleet Oiler RFA *Tidespring* with M Company on board, a naval gunfire support team, a SBS section and D Squadron SAS on the Fleet Replenishment Ship *Fort Austin*. Sheridan had the experience he needed within the M Company Group and did not need the SAS, but he was overruled. Intelligence believed South Georgia was defended by a Marine platoon with a potential reserve from Constantino Davidoff's employees. There were no reports suggesting the Argentines had contacted the British Antarctic Survey field parties and two women wildlife photographers known to be ashore. Winter was approaching.

Heading south after departing from Ascension, CTG 317.9 met HMS *Endurance* heading north from the Falklands and replenished her. Sheridan was unaware that during the resupply, D Squadron had cross-decked to her. A SBS section transferred from the submarine HMS *Conqueror*, which had conducted a coastal recce of South Georgia on 18 April. Two days later, an RAF Victor flying from Ascension conducted a 150,000 square miles Maritime Radar Reconnaissance, collecting information on shipping, weather, icebergs and sea state

Detailing orders, Sheridan ordered 2 SBS to land at Hound Bay and collect intelligence for M Company to attack Grytviken, the principal target. 19 (Mountain) Troop was to attack Leith about 9 miles to the north. He ordered glaciers were to be avoided. However, Sheridan was unaware that the SAS were using their Satellite Communications to consult with two SAS, who had climbed Mount Everest in 1976, about landing on Fortuna Glacier. The pair had never been to South Georgia. Nevertheless air photographs were examined and the glacier was judged to be suitable. Captain Young rejected the concerns of Major Sheridan and the expert regional knowledge of Captain Barker, commanding HMS *Endurance*, that the option was unwise. Operation *Paraquet,* a small parrot, had metamorphosed into Operation *Paraquat*, the weed killer! Atrocious weather during the morning of 21 April prevented the insertion of 19 Troop until a short spell in the early afternoon allowed a helicopter to land them. A deep front then forced the Troop into a night of surviving. The following morning, three anti-submarine Wessex helicopters stripped for the assault reached the SAS, but two crashed and third helicopter, the Wessex-3 anti-submarine helicopter nicknamed 'Humphrey', flew the entire Troop to *Antrim*. Rejection of expert advice had placed Operation *Paraquet* at risk.

Shortly after midnight on 23 April, 17 (Boat) Troop SAS, under orders to observe Leith from Green Island, launched from *Antrim* in five Rigid Gemini inflatables in reasonably calm seas, but none were tethered and two Geminis were separated in the brisk offshore breeze. Captain Young was then alerted to the Argentine submarine *Santa Fe*, a Second World War veteran, entering Cumberland Bay East to the east of Grytviken and her presence dominated naval operations. The submarine commanding officer had seen *Endurance* but did not attack because he knew her captain. Young ordered *Tidespring* with M Company embarked to leave the South Georgia Maritime Exclusion Zone, which reduced the size of Sheridan's force. A patrolling Argentine Boeing-707 spotted *Endurance* recovering the SBS in Hound Bay. The six missing SAS were later rescued. Meanwhile, the *Santa Fe* had landed a 1st Marine Infantry platoon at Grytviken but was attacked by helicopters on the surface and limped back to Grytviken. Although the assault force had been reduced, Sheridan was ordered by Captain Young to capture Grytviken and during the helicopter assault, D Squadron was held up by 'enemy' that turned out to be a colony of elephant seals. Leith was also captured and about 150 Argentines were interned on the *Tidespring*. Captain Young signalled Northwood: 'Be pleased to inform Her Majesty that the White ensign flies alongside the Union Jack on South Georgia. God save the Queen.'

As British resolve hardened, President Galtieri needed a strong negotiation stance and on 26th April, the day after South Georgia was lost, Brigadier-General Omar Parada and his 3rd Mechanised Infantry Brigade based in northern sub-tropical province of Corrientes was ordered to transfer to the chilly Falklands. Parada summoned his reservists by radio and television announcements, newspapers, phone calls and telegrams and home visits instructing them to join the troop train trundling to the southern port of Puerto Deseado. However, a shortfall forced him to include men conscripted in January. The ship carrying equipment then hit a rock and returned for repairs. As reinforcements then arrived using the 'Air Bridge' to Stanley, there was congestion and since there was no accommodation, the troops, many away from home for the first time, camped in the cold wind and rain and without transport then had long marches to their deployment areas carrying almost all their equipment and stores and then had to dig in. Morale was not high. To replace 3rd Artillery Group attached to 10th Brigade on the Falklands, he was given the 4th Airborne Artillery Group from the National Strategic Reserve. Falklands Military Garrison was reformed into two tactical areas of operations:

**Army Group Stanley – Brigadier-General Jofre**
Defence of Stanley – 10th Brigade.
>   4th Regiment and 5th Marine infantry Battalion.

>   Z Strategic Reserve. Combat Team *Solari* (B Company, 12th Infantry Regiment) on Mount Kent as the Air Mobile Reserve.

Military Air Base Stanley.

**Army Group Litoral – Brigadier-General Parada**
9th Brigade disbanded. Defence transferred to 3rd Brigade.

**East Falkland**
>   Task Force *Mercedes* at Goose Green of two 12th Infantry Regiment companies and a 25th Infantry Regiment company.

Military Air Base Goose Green.

**West Falkland**
>   5th and 8th Infantry Regiments.

As the news that the Task Force was en route to the Falklands spread, Civil Affairs announced a war footing on 27 April. Shops in Stanley were to close by 4 p.m. A curfew and blackout was imposed daily between 6 p.m. and 6.30 a.m. Major Dowling increased his internal security operations and when 181 Military Company arrested several men and boys, Wing-Commander Bloomer-Reeve instructed Navy Captain Hussey to inform Dowling that his attitude was undermining community relations and he was clearly incapable of identifying the difference between Internal Security and conventional operations. Dowling retorted that the problem was trying to 'win' over a hostile population, a remark that saw him sent back to Argentina within days. Brigadier Parada had planned to move his Brigade HQ to Goose Green, however his radios and equipment was still in Argentina on the damaged ship and inter-service rivalry saw Air Force HQ contriving to disrupt his plans. When the 12th Infantry Regiment arrived at Goose Green, Lieutenant-Colonel Italo Piaggi, the Commanding Officer, met Wing-Commander Wilson Pedrozo, commanding the Air Force base, who insisted that he was senior by date of commission, he should command the defence of Goose Green. The military regime hardened. When Second-Lieutenant Centurion demanded provisions from the Farm Store and Goss insisted he sign and commented that logistics must be chaotic if soldiers were expected to fight without adequate rations, Centurion told him not to be so cheeky. Next day, Centurion complained that the Jetty Warehouse was cold and demanded warmer accommodation. Goss again antagonised him, 'What sort of war have you come to fight? First no rations and now no tents or bivouac bags.' The agitated Centurion again threatened, 'Your cheek will get you shot'. When the Argentines suggested the soldiers be billeted among the community, Goss was keen to avoid them being billeted among the 'kelper' and offered four empty houses in Goose Green, two in Darwin and Darwin Boarding School midway between the two settlements. Classes were relocated.

Task Force warships tightened the siege on the 30th. The Maritime Exclusion Zone was converted into the Total Exclusion Zone and extended to apply to 'any ships and any aircraft'. Prime Minister Thatcher repeated there could be no negotiations until Argentina withdrew. Next day, the 50 Squadron Vulcan bomber XM 607 departed from Ascension and, supported by a relay of Victor tankers, headed south on the first of five Operation *Black Buck* raids to bomb Military Air Base Stanley. An electrical storm interrupted the last of the outward refuels. Nevertheless the pilot, Flight-Lieutenant Martin Withers, insisted, 'We are short on fuel, but we have come this far. I'm not turning back now'. Dropping below radar during the final approach, he opened the air war by releasing twenty-two bombs and then climbed in the expectation of anti-aircraft fire. He was unaware that Argentine air defence had concluded his Vulcan to be friendly. Although air photographs showed one bomb had hit the runway, the psychological pressure on the Argentines was priceless. On the same day, in the first air-to-air engagement, two Sea Harriers shot down two Air Force Mirage IIIAs. Destroyers began a programme of bombarding Army Group Stanley at night.

During the day, three RAF Harriers attacked Goose Green. Lieutenant-Colonel Piaggi interned the seventy-two adults and forty-three children, a total of 115 people including some from Darwin and about twenty refugees from Stanley, into the Community Hall and were advised Lieutenant-Colonel Piaggi would visit. The internees included a baby aged four months and three octogenarians. A conscript was placed on the entrance. No food was supplied until after dark when a friendly Argentine air force sergeant was persuaded to allow the internees a discreet 'shop' at the Farm Store. As with all prisoners, the internees soon developed subterfuge to exploit every opportunity, usually after dark, to collect food, blankets and pillows. Willy Bowles was the prime interface with the Argentines. By trade a carpenter, he built an air-raid shelter underneath the Community Hall floor and provided a shelter for Nancy McCullum, aged eighty-two.

The International Committee of the Red Cross (ICRC) was formed in 1929 as a neutral intermediary during hostilities and by 1982 had developed four conventions:

1. Treatment of wounded and sick of armed forces on the battlefield.
2. Needs of sick, wounded, and shipwrecked members of armed forces at sea.
3. Treatment of prisoners of war.
4. Protection of civilians.

While there was a historical relationship between UK and the ICRC, Argentina largely ignored its principles until an ICRC delegation demanded to inspect the welfare of those confined to the Community Hall. The inspectors were unimpressed. There was no nominal role of internees, the Community Hall was not marked or registered as an internment camp, sanitation was not checked, no blankets were supplied and no medical visits had taken place. Believing that several radio transmissions had originated from Goose Green, the Community Hall was raided on several occasions. Bob Mcleod and another radio amateur, Ray Robson, had coaxed an old wireless and listening the BBC World

Service was screened by people chattering loudly in the bar. Lieutenant-Colonel Piaggi eventually visited and when he appointed a Captain Sanchez to supervise the internees, there were immediate improvements. A medical officer regularly visited, several women prepared meals in the Galley, and a shepherd allowed to check his flock with his dogs found that hungry soldiers had stolen some mutton. A shepherd using a motorcycle and dog to check on his sheep on Goat Rincon was intercepted by an Army Puma helicopter, flown to Goose Green and confined to a chair outside the Galley until Goss negotiated his release. Several detainees, including Brook Hardcastle and Mr and Mrs Goss, were released to their houses in the middle of the month,

At sea, an Argentine Navy attempt to trap the Carrier Task Group in a pincer north-east of the Falklands on 2 May, resulting in HMS *Conqueror* torpedoing the elderly Argentine cruiser *General Belgrano*. Launched in 1933 and survivor of the Japanese attack on Pearl Harbour in 1941, the 323 seamen who died was about 50 per cent of the total Argentines killed during the war. As Admiral Anaya had predicted, the Argentine Navy remained in port for the rest of the war. Sea Harriers sank a fast patrol boat and damaged a Falkland Islands Company coaster requisitioned as an auxiliary. Argentina had not signed the US embargo against the Soviet Union for its invasion of Afghanistan and using satellite information, on 4th May, Super Etendards of the Navy 2nd Squadron sank HMS *Sheffield* with an Exocet missile, the first Royal Navy warship lost in action since 1945. On the same day, Lieutenant-Commander Nick Taylor RN, of 800 Naval Air Squadron, was killed in a low level raid on Military Air Base Condor at Goose Green. SBS patrols began reconnoitring assault beaches and the SAS established inland patrols. After a naval bombardment of shore-based targets by the Royal Navy, Civil Affairs surveyed houses in Stanley suitable for shelters.

Strong suspicions in early May that Argentine eavesdropping was monitoring the Falklands R/T network emerged when HMS *Hermes* started Psychological Warfare broadcasts, usually after Doctor's Hour. Inevitably, the subject attracted radio chatter among the farms and Robin Pitulaga, the owner of San Salvador, agreed to respond. Two Puma helicopters carrying commandos raided the farm and then detained Pitulaga and flew him to Moody Brook, arriving in the middle of a naval bombardment of Army Group Stanley. At Stanley Police Station, Pitulaga experienced 'Mutt', the aggressive military police officer, and 'Jeff', the reasonable one suggesting he write a statement, which was ripped up. Placed in a cell, he was joined by a dozen local men arrested in a pub after breaching curfew. At about midnight, he was marched to Victory Green by a captain threatening to execute him and confined overnight to a trench occupied by two nervous conscripts. Next day, Bloomer-Reeve ordered his release to the Upland Goose Hotel where his sister was married to the owner, Desmond King, where remained until the Argentine surrender.

Meanwhile, a small convoy that included the P&O Roll-On/Roll-Off Ferry MV *Norland* carrying 2 Para joined the Amphibious Task Group at Ascension on 7 May, having left UK on 26 April. The Argentine Navy had converted several trawlers for intelligence gathering and on the 9th, the SBS boarded the *Narwhal*, a freezer trawler, and captured a naval intelligence officer and substantial information. A group of Falklanders led by Mario Zuvic, of Chilean-Yugoslavian extraction and an expert in electronics, jammed and cloned Argentine communications, including Advanced Observer Posts equipped with radios confiscated from Falkland Islanders deployed around the coast on early warning. Intercept of 'Naval Air Base Cauldron' in Argentine communications led to HQ Land

Forces ordering the SAS to check four possible locations by 15 May. On 11/12 May, D Squadron raided the last option of Naval Auxiliary Airstrip Calderon on Pebble Island being used by six Naval Air Beechcraft T-34C Mentor trainers and also several Air Force Pucaras diverted by weather from Stanley and Goose Green. The Navy had moved to Pebble Island because they were fed up with bickering Air Force pilots. A 3rd Marine Infantry Battalion platoon providing the defence thought the raid was naval gunfire. Several aircraft were destroyed and damaged. Next morning, the Argentines accused the Islanders of sabotaging the aircraft and confined them to the Farm Manager's house.

The approach of winter and weak distribution of supplies was affecting Argentine units based in warmer climates; for instance, Task Force *Reconquest* (8th Regiment) at Fox Bay had a sick list of over 200.

Apart from media reports, Argentina had very little intelligence on the activity on Ascension. The Empresa Lineas Maritimas Argentina freighter *Rio de la Plata* (10,409 tons) was noted lurking offshore and withdrew.

South Georgia. Operation Paraquet, 22 April. D Squadron load a Wessex helicopter for deployment to Fortuna Glacier. Their rescue next day cost two Wessex anti-submarine helicopters.

Operation *Paraquet*, 25 April. Captain Chris Nunn, who commanded M Company, 42 Commando, on HMS *Antrim* Flight Deck. This photo is often claimed to show SAS, including by the BBC *Antiques Roadshow*. (Major Sheridan).

Lieutenant-Commander Astiz surrenders on HMS *Plymouth*. While the 150 prisoners were repatriated through Montevideo, Astiz was sent to the UK to help police with inquiries into the murders of nationals foreign during the 'Dirty War'. Released on 10 June without charge, he was later sentenced to life in Argentina.

M Company, 42 Commando, guard prisoners at Leith.

Ascension. The first air raid was launched from RAF Wideawake on 1 May when a Vulcan supported by relays of Victor in-flight refuellers. Also on the pad are Nimrod maritime recce aircraft and Harriers.

*Above left*: The bombing led to the Argentines and local representatives organising civil defence in Stanley and several robust houses were designated Defence Aerea Pasiva (Passive Air Defence) shelters.

*Above right*: Argentine positions came under regular naval bombardment from warships offshore and air attacks resulting in damage and guns being moved.

The 'Bleeding Helmet'. Navy Lieutenant Carlos Benitez had gone to investigate a ship, however he crashed in poor visibility while returning to Stanley Military Air Base and was buried in Stanley Cemetery. His helmet was placed on his commemorative wooden cross and every time it rained, water dripping from a leather chin strap left streak deposits or 'tears'. (Eduardo Rotondo)

South Atlantic. HMS *Fearless*. When the Amphibious Task Force departed from Ascension on radio silence, stores, information and intelligence were dropped by RAF C-130 Hercules and collected by the ship's boats. (Author)

South Atlantic. Refuelling at sea (RASing). HMS *Fearless* and a RFA Fleet Replenishment Ship refuel from a RFA tanker. The Royal Navy was one of the few fleets in which all replenishment was passed alongside, as opposed to ships in line astern. (Author)

South Atlantic. HMS *Fearless* replenishing from a Fleet Replenishment Ship using a jackstay - a light running block – used to transfer personnel and light stores to a maximum load of about 250 kg. (Author)

In addition to Argentine Air Force Boeing-707s transport squadrons diverted to conduct maritime recce. Argentina could also rely on sightings reported by Soviet Air Force Tupolev-95 BEAR D strategic bombers flying between Angola and Cuba, sometimes at low level.

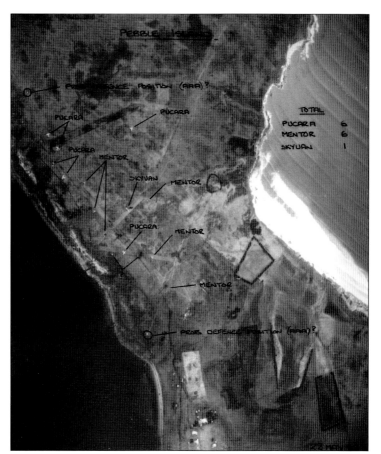

*Right*: Pebble Island. Air photograph of Naval Air Base Cauldron after the SAS raid on 15 May indicating eleven aircraft damaged. The base was defended by a 3rd Marine Infantry Battalion company. (Crown Copyright)

*Below*: MAP H. 15 May. HQ 3 Commando Brigade Intelligence estimate of Argentine positions.

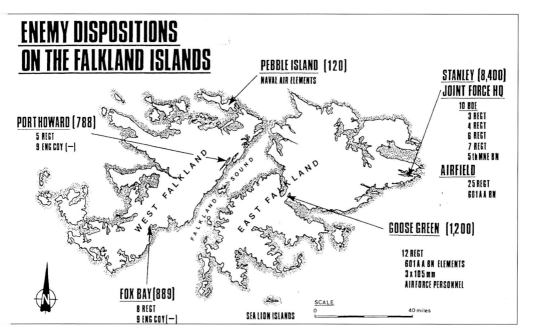

# ENEMY DISPOSITIONS
# ON THE FALKLAND ISLANDS

**PEBBLE ISLAND (120)**
NAVAL AIR ELEMENTS

**STANLEY (8,400)**
**JOINT FORCE HQ**
10 BDE
3 REGT
4 REGT
6 REGT
7 REGT
5th MNE BN

**AIRFIELD**
25 REGT
601 AA BN

**PORT HOWARD (788)**
5 REGT
9 ENG COY (−)

**GOOSE GREEN (1,200)**
12 REGT
601 AA BN ELEMENTS
3 x 105mm
AIRFORCE PERSONNEL

**FOX BAY (889)**
8 REGT
9 ENG COY (−)

WEST FALKLAND

EAST FALKLAND

FALKLAND SOUND

SEA LION ISLANDS

SCALE
0          40 miles

Desde las

20 a las 23 horas

R.A.S.

Frequencia

9,71 MHz

**RADIO ATLANTICO DEL SUR**

Aviso a los habitantes de las Islas Malvinas

Tengo el gran placer de anunciarles una nueva emisora radial.

Radio Atlántico del Sur transmitirá a diario desde las 20 a las 23 horas en frecuencia de 9,71 MHz.

Esta transmisión operará como una emisora adicional a la LRA Radio Nacional Malvinas.

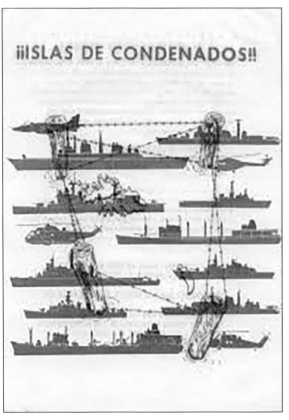

¡¡¡ISLAS DE CONDENADOS!!

*Above left*: Psychological Warfare pamphlet introducing Radio South Atlantic between 8 p.m. and 11 p.m. nightly to Army Group Falklands – front.

*Above right*: Psychological Warfare pamphlet introducing Radio South Atlantic to Army Group Falklands – reverse. (Crown Copyright)

*Left*: Psychological Warfare pamphlet translated as The Condemned Isle. (Crown Copyright)

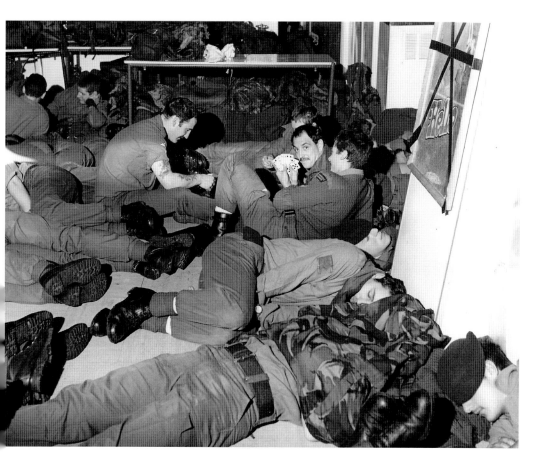

*Above*: 19 May. 40 Commando on board HMS *Fearless* after being transferred from *Canberra*.

*Right*: 19 May. As HMS *Fearless* went to Action Stations, the 'galleys' were extinguished' and Combat Messing of a bread roll and mug of stew were introduced.

# Chapter 7

# Operation *Sutton*: Landings at San Carlos Water

On 11 May, Major-General Moore signalled Brigadier Thompson on HMS *Fearless*:

> You are to secure a bridgehead on East Falkland, into which reinforcements can be landed, in which an airstrip can be established and from which operations to repossess the Falkland Islands can be achieved.
>
> You are to push forward from the bridgehead area so far as the maintenance of its security allows, to gain information, to establish moral and physical domination over the enemy and to forward the ultimate objectives of repossession.
>
> You will retain operational control of all forces in the Falklands until I establish my Headquarters in the area. It is my intention to do this, aboard HMS Fearless, as early as practicable after the landing. I expect this to be approximately on D+7.
>
> It is then my intention to land 5 Infantry Brigade into the beachhead and develop operations for the complete repossession of the Falklands.

Next day, the Cunard liner *Queen Elizabeth Two* departed from Southampton with an Embarked Force that included 5th Infantry Brigade. Lieutenant-General Sir Richard Trant moved to Northwood as Deputy Commander Land Forces. He had previously commanded Army rapid response operations outside NATO. Keenly anticipated in the same convoy was the container ship *Atlantic Conveyor* carrying six Wessex HU-5s and four CH-47 Chinook assault helicopters.

Argentine intelligence assessed the British would adopt a favourable political bargaining position by capturing as much of the Stanley peninsula as possible either by direct assault against Army Group Stanley or an amphibious assault north-east in the North Camp area. Berkeley Sound was regarded as the likely option because its occupation could be achieved with minimum casualties and be favourable to British public opinion. Special Forces incursions, electronic surveillance and naval bombardment were anticipated.

On the 12th, Thompson issued his Orders for Operation *Sutton*, the codename for the landings. He began, 'Mission. To land at Port San Carlos, San Carlos and Ajax Bay and to establish a beachhead for mounting offensive operations leading to the recapture of the Falkland Islands.' San Carlos Water was in the middle of the Argentine occupation and had been disregarded by the Argentines as suitable for a landing because of the distance to Stanley, about 60 miles. 3 Commando Brigade was to defend the beachhead and wait for 5th Infantry Brigade, unless an opportunity to advance to Stanley arose. The Argentines were expected to counter-attack. The design for battle was 'a silent night attack by landing craft with the object of securing all high ground by first light'. The SBS had reconnoitred several beaches and exits. The sixteen landing craft on HMS *Fearless* and *Intrepid* would lead the assault and Brigade HQ would control troop helicopters, artillery and naval gunfire. A terrain brief and intelligence assessment was followed by Thompson detailing his plan for landing and defence of the San Carlos Water beachhead:

First wave 3.30 a.m. (local)
2 Para. Land on *Red Beach* (Ajax Bay) *and* consolidate on Sussex Mountain to secure the southern flank.

40 Commando and a Blues and Royals troop. Land on *Blue Beach* (San Carlos) and secure the beachhead eastern flank.

Second wave 7.30 a.m.
45 Commando. Land on *Red Beach*. Seize the derelict refrigeration plant and secure Sussex Mountain and the western flank.

3 Para and a Blues and Royals troop. Land at *Green Beach* (Port San Carlos) and secure the northern flank.

Floating Reserve
42 Commando. On *Canberra*.

Artillery
29 Commando Regiment Group and the T (*Shah Shujah*) Battery Rapiers to be flown ashore as a high priority.

148 Commando Forward Observation Battery direct naval gunfire.

Logistics
Commando Logistic Regiment. Establish ammunition dump, stores and hospital at *Red Beach*.

Diversions
D Squadron. Convince Task Force *Mercedes* that a regiment was attacking – 'noise, firepower but no close engagement'.

HMS *Glamorgan*. Keep Army Group Stanley focused on Berkeley Sound.

Major John Chester, the Brigade Chief-of-Staff, giving the detail mentioned, with a wry smile, that in British amphibious operations, H-Hour was the time when the first landing craft beached and L-Hour was the touchdown time for the first wave of helicopter assaults. Simple to remember, he said 'H' was for landing craft and 'L' for helicopters!' The date and time of D-Day was a political decision; the first opportunity was between 16 and 25 May. After questions, Brigadier Thompson concluded, 'May I remind you that this will be no picnic. Good luck and stay flexible!' He later wrote a book about 3 Commando Brigade in the Falklands entitled *No Picnic*.

During the afternoon, Northwood reported that the Argentines had deployed Combat Team (CT) *Guemes* (*Eagle)* from Goose Green to Port San Carlos. While its purpose was not clear, an Argentine combat team usually implied a company. Its Command Post was identified at Port San Carlos and it was commanded by First-Lieutenant Esteban, from Goose Green. Under his command was an infantry company with support weapons and logistic support from 12th and 25th Infantry Regiments. A platoon identified on Fanning Head was nicknamed the 'Fanning Hill Mob'. Documents captured on D-Day described its role was 'to block and control the entrance to San Carlos Water and to observe for enemy naval activity and possible landings at Port Howard, Fox Bay and Darwin'. Although compromise of Operation *Sutton* was thought unlikely, Brigadier Thompson responded to the intelligence by adjusting the landing plan to *Blue* and *Red Beaches* being seized simultaneously:

First wave
2 Para. Land on *Blue Beach One* and block any enemy approaches from Goose Green by occupying Sussex Mountain.

40 Commando. Land on *Blue Beach One*.

Second wave
45 Commando. Land on the *Red Beach* at Ajax Bay.
3 Para. Land at *Green Beach* and secure Port San Carlos.

Fanning Head
3 SBS. Neutralise the 'Fanning Head Mob'.

Some Royal Marines were less than impressed that their traditional 'first ashore role' had been usurped by the Parachute Regiment.

Commodore Clapp had planned the landing and then on the 18th, Northwood ordered that no two major infantry units were to be on the same ship. It was fortunate that as the Amphibious Task Group loitered outside the north-eastern sector of the Total Exclusion Zone waiting for the authorization of Operation *Sutton*, the South Atlantic was sufficiently calm for landing craft and helicopters to transfer 40 Commando and 3 Para to *Fearless* and *Intrepid* respectively. However, a Sea King carrying SAS ditched with the loss of twenty-one lives after a bird strike.

Meanwhile, such had been concerns at Northwood that Argentina was assessed to have three Exocets that HQ SAS was tasked to raid Air Force Base Rio Grande in southern Argentina and destroy them in Operation *Mikado*. Early on 17 May, in the first phase, Operation *Plum Duff*, eight SAS landed in a stripped-down Sea King HC-3 to recce the airfield; however, there was thick fog, the Argentines were alert and destroying the helicopter proved difficult. Nevertheless, its three aircrew and the SAS crossed separately into Chile and contacted the British Embassy. It later emerged the Argentines had reinforced the defence with four Marine Corps battalions. The failure led to the Security Intelligence Service scouring the market for Exocets.

Intelligence gathered from debriefs included that Argentine soldiers listened to programmes on small short-wave transistors and that the BBC Spanish Language and World Services were highly regarded. The Argentine Armed Forces *Radio Liberty* was nicknamed by the British as *Argentine Annie*. Radio as a persuasive medium to spread information and undermine morale was well known but when the Psychological Operations Section at the National Defence College examined options a week after the Argentine invasion, three issues emerged. First, Psychological Operations had never been asked to address Argentine attitudes to British interests in the South Atlantic. Secondly, the delivery of leaflets fired from field artillery and dropping from aircraft had been largely discontinued. Thirdly, there was insufficient Spanish linguists. In late April, the Ministry of Defence launched Operation *Moonshine* and hired a transmitter at Ascension for voice and jamming. Within three weeks, *Radio Atlántico del Sur* (Radio South Atlantic) was formed and managed by an experienced station manager. In support were Spanish speakers from within the Armed Forces as announcers, translators and typists; two experienced news editors; a civilian radio engineer and two RAF technicians checking the quality of broadcasts and transmission; three Intelligence Corps corporals plotting the battle picture; and co-ordinators and librarians. The Cabinet approved *Radio Atlántico del Sur* and on 18 May, leaflets were delivered to Falklands Military Garrison highlighting nightly broadcasts from 10 p.m. to 2 a.m. daily. Attempts to jam programmes confirmed there was considerable concern. At Goose Green, transistors used by Argentine conscripts were destroyed and the military chaplain Father Fernandez warned that listening was a mortal sin. The Junta closed the Argentine Press Agency on 1 June for three days when it listed casualties and prisoners nightly collected from *Radio Atlántico del Sur*. It also emerged from listener feedback that Latin American countries did not approve of Argentina and *Radio Atlántico del Sur* was trusted. Argentina later closed down its *Radio Nacional Malvinas* leaving *Radio Atlántico del Sur* the only station available to Argentine servicemen.

Political authority for Operation *Sutton* was passed to Brigadier Thompson with D-Day being Friday 21 May, H-Hour at 3.30 a.m. and 8.30 a.m. for the landings to be secure. After dark on the 20th, the Amphibious Task Group loitering around the TEZ went to Action Stations and set a course toward the north-east coast of East Falkland and then diverted to Falkland Sound and arrived undetected outside San Carlos Water about midnight. The SBS neutralised the 'Fanning Hill Mob' and the SAS watched Task Force *Mercedes* at Goose Green. 40 Commando landed on *Blue Beach* at San Carlos and was welcomed by Mr Pat Short, the Farm Manager, with 'Oh! You're here. We wondered when you were going to come'. His wife, Isabel, broadcast on the CB 'We've just received a lot of friends!' 2 Para landed on *Red Beach* and occupied Sussex Mountain to block incursions from Goose Green. 45 Commando also landed on *Blue Beach* alongside 2 Para. Alan Miller, the Port San Carlos Farm Manager, heard shelling of Fanning Head and, climbing to high ground with a friend, saw landing craft delivering 3 Para to *Green Beach*. Combat Team *Guemes*, withdrawing from Port San Carlos, shot down three 3 Commando Brigade Air Squadron Gazelle helicopters.

The Commando Logistic Regiment at the end of an 8,000-mile logistic thread from Plymouth landed on *Red Beach* and, occupying the derelict refrigeration plant, began distributing supplies, repaired equipment and treated casualties at the Field Hospital, including several Argentines captured during the landings being the first. 42 Commando remained in reserve. San Carlos Water quickly became a battleground as the Argentine Air Force and Naval Air Command attacked the ships. The two Argentine regiments on West Falkland had been isolated.

At about midday, Squadron-Leader Bob Iveson and Flight-Lieutenant Jeff Glover of 1 (Fighter) Squadron, both flying RAF Harrier GR3s, were tasked to carry out a low-level air photographic reconnaissance of Port Howard. After Iveson aborted when his Harrier undercarriage failed, Glover made his first pass without attracting ground fire. Instructed to make a second pass, he allowed the Argentines about ten minutes to relax and started his run, but his Harrier was hit from the ground and as it rolled and a wing folded, he detonated the explosive cable around his cockpit canopy and ejected. He was quite low and with his parachute partially deployed, he hit the water hard. His immersion suit keeping him afloat, he released the parachute and inflated his dinghy and was picked up by several soldiers from 601 Commando Company using a rowing boat. Ashore, Captain Santiago Llanos, a Marine Corps medical officer, took Glover as the pillion on a motorcycle, and with two soldiers running alongside to prevent him falling off, took Glover to the Social Club where he dressed his broken arm, shoulder and collar bone. Next day, he took him by helicopter to Goose Green where he introduced Glover to the soldier credited with shooting him down with a Blowpipe surface-to-air missile. Glover was flown to Stanley and then joined other casualties, including Argentine pilots, in C-130 Hercules casualty evacuation flight to Comodoro Rivadavia Military Air Base. After further treatment at the Base hospital, he was confined to the Officers' Mess, visited by several officers and experienced casual interrogation. After several days, he was taken to another air base where he faced some hostility but no violence. In early June, he was sent to a military hospital in Buenos Aries for further treatment.

Next evening, two 800 Squadron Sea Harriers forced the naval patrol craft *Rio Iguaza*, en route to Goose Green carrying three 105mm Pack Howitzers from the 4th Artillery Airborne Battery allocated to join Task Force *Mercedes*, to beach about halfway in Choiseul Sound. The Argentines recovered two guns. The third gun was damaged and replaced by a fourth gun in the Battery.

After withdrawing from Port San Carlos on D-Day, the surviving Combat Team *Guemes* reached Douglas on 23 May where First-Lieutenant Esteban confined the Islanders to the Community Hall and demanded a Land Rover take two of his men to Port Stanley. However, this broke down and the two soldiers asked to use a tractor from David Barton, the Teal Inlet Farm Manager. They reached Estancia on the next day and met a patrol from the Air Mobile Reserve (Combat Team *Solari*) on Mount Kent. However, a helicopter to Stanley was not available and so the two soldiers returned to Douglas. Esteban decided to use the tractor to drive to Stanley and although Tony Heathman, the Estancia Farm Manager, described the route, within about an hour, the tractor was bogged down and the tide was flooding. Esteban was impatient and next morning, Heathman drove them to Teal where Rex McKay, a shepherd, drove them to Douglas where they were collected by a helicopter and flown to Stanley.

*Right*: MAP I. Approach to San Carlos Water.

*Below left*: MAP J. San Carlos Beach Head.

*Below right*: MAP K. Ministry of Defence Intelligence debriefed members of the public who had been repatriated and sent the results 'down south'. Patrick Burnstein was interviewed about San Carlos, which became *Blue Beach*.

## APPROACH TO SAN CARLOS WATERS

TEZ

200 Miles

Amphibious task force enter 200800 ź may

Entered assault area 210130 ź may

Approx 2300 ź hrs altered course for approach

Course set for Port Stanley daylight hours

Altered course after last light

N

NOTES
1. Entered TEZ 0800 ź 20 May 82
Sea conditions bad

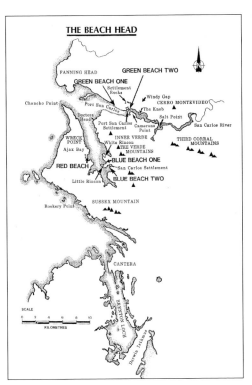

THE BEACH HEAD

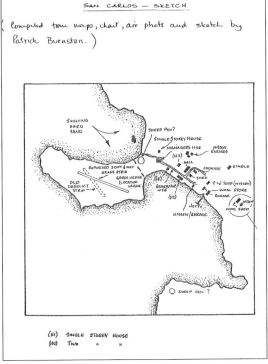

SAN CARLOS — SKETCH

( Compiled from maps, chart, air photos and sketch by Patrick Burnsten. )

Early on 21 May (day), before the air raids began. HMS *Fearless* with the entrance to San Carlos Water and Fanning Head in the distance. Astern is *Canberra* and in the air is a 3 Commando Brigade Air Squadron Scout helicopter. The 7.62 mm machine-gun is in a temporary fitting. (Crown Copyright)

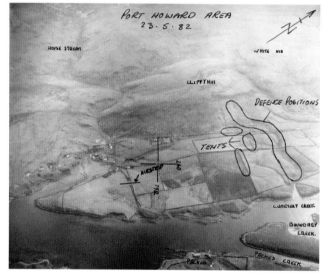

West Falkland. Air photo of Port Howard dated 23 May. The garrison was occupied by 5th Infantry Regiment. With the 8th Infantry Brigade at Fox Bay, it provided the defence of West Falkland. Both suffered from ineffective logistics.

21 May, Port Howard. Flt-Lt Glover being helped by an Argentine commando after being shot down near Port Howard. He was held as a prisoner of war.

After withdrawing from Port San Carlos, during which they shot down three Gazelle helicopters on 21 May, Lt Estaban and Combat Team Guemes reached Stanley. Most then reinforced Task Forces Mercedes at Goose Green on 28 May and were captured.

May 20. A-4Q Skyhawks Navy pilots at Air Base Rio Grande.

*Green Beach.* A sergeant captured on 22 May by 3 Para near Port San Carlos was the first prisoner. He had been with Combat Team Guemes at Fanning Head.

*Above*: Developed for the US Navy and Marine Corps and first flown in 1954, A-4 Skyhawks had a bomb load equivalent to a Second World War B-17 bomber and were first sold to Argentina in 1974.

*Left*: San Carlos Water was regularly attacked. This raid is on D+3 (23 May). (Chris Baxter)

*Blue Beaches One* and *Two* at San Carlos D+1 (22 May). (Author)

*Above*: *Blue Beach*, San Carlos, 22 May. (Author)

*Right*: *Blue Beach*. HQ 3 Commando Brigade dug in and covered by camouflage dark green nets. A person leaves using the entrance.

*Blue Beach*. A bunker of 3 Commando Brigade HQ and Signal Squadron supported Brigade HQ with communications and logistic support. (Crown Copyright)

*Blue Beach*, San Carlos. *Fearless* LCU lands vehicles, including a BV 202 and Land Rover, and equipment. In the background is a meat hanging frame. (Author)

*Red Beach*, Ajax Bay. Used by the Commando Logistic Regiment to support the distribution of supplies, manage the field hospital and repair equipment.

*Green Beach*. Port San Carlos, 23 May. Manhandling stores from a *Fearless* LCU.

*Right: Red Beach*. Unloading a Mexefloat motorised ferry.

*Below*: 24 May. *Intrepid* LCU at *Blue Beach*. Ashore is a Centurion Armoured Recovery tank. On the beach is a 1 Raiding Squadron, Royal Marines Rigid Raider.

*Bottom*: *Red Beach*. Fires after an air raid.

San Carlos Water, 23 May. HMS *Antelope* was hit by two bombs (dark mark on hull) and 'Abandon Ship' was ordered. Of two Army bomb disposal NCOs who attempted to defuse the bombs, one was killed and the second was severely wounded when one exploded. Both were experienced in defusing terrorist bombs, but not naval ordnance.

San Carlos Water, morning of 24 May. The pall of white smoke from burning aluminium on *Antelope* and clear skies was a beacon for air raids. (Author)

San Carlos Water. *Antelope* has broken in half during the morning and later sinks.

Some units encouraged a daily 'Doctors Call'. At *Blue Beach*, a RN medic, carrying a small pack, attached to 3 Commando Brigade HQ and Signals Squadron, visits positions. An *Intrepid* LCU heads for *Blue Beach One* in the background.

*Right: Red Beach*. The 'Red and Green Life Machine' Field Hospital commanded by Surgeon-Lieutenant Rick Jolly (with a beard).

*Below*: Her Majesty's Hospital Ship *Uganda* was refitted as a general hospital with departments that included Casualty Reception, Operating Theatres, Intensive Care, X-Ray, laboratories and rehabiliation.

*Above*: ARA *Almirante Irizar*, an ice-breaker and naval transport converted to a hospital ship, collecting Argentine casualties from Stanley after the surrender.

*Left*: The *Atlantic Conveyor*, a requisitioned roll-on/roll-off transport carrying fuel and ammunition below decks and six Westland Wessexes, three CH-47 Chinooks and a Lynx helicopter on the upper deck was abandoned on 25 May after being hit by two Exocets fired by two Argentine Navy Super Etendards. A Chinook and a Wessex were saved. Twelve men died including the Master, Captain Ian North, who was posthumously awarded the DSC. He had served on the Atlantic convoys during the Second World War. The last ship to be sunk by enemy action was in 1945.

The surviving Chinook HC-1 ZA 718, known as *Bravo November*, played a crucial role in moving artillery, ammunition and stores forward. It had survived the sinking because it was airborne and achieved a heroic reputation as the only heavy lift helicopter.

Darwin Boarding School. Commemoration for an Argentine sailor killed when the Naval Patrol Craft *Rio Iguaza* was attacked by a Harrier in Choiseul Sound on 22 May while ferrying 105 mm Pack Howitzers for Task Force Mercedes at Goose Green.

30 May. *Intrepid* LCU landing a Scots Guard company.

# Chapter 8

# The Break-Out From San Carlos Water

The Junta strategy was to isolate 3 Commando Brigade by sinking both British aircraft-carriers and attacking the Ascension logistic chain. There was no intelligence to suggest that Falklands Military Garrison was planning to counter-attack the beachhead and no further indication the Argentine Navy had left port.

Countermanding Major-General Moore's 11 May directive, on 23 May, Admiral Fieldhouse ordered Thompson to 'establish moral and physical domination over the enemy' and added he did not need artillery. Brigade intelligence suggested there was no evidence of Task Force *Mercedes* counter-attacking the beachhead. Thompson had planned that D Squadron and 42 Commando would seize Mount Kent and support a brigade advance to Stanley but now altered his plan to 2 Para attacking Goose Green because it was the nearest enemy. The arrival of the *Atlantic Conveyor* and its supplies and helicopters was imminent. However, convoy defence failed to prevent its abandoning on the 25th when it was hit by two Exocet missiles and sank with the helicopters three days later. Thompson rejected the alternative of using the surviving helicopter force to support an advance on foot and decided to consolidate around San Carlos Water, amid the air raids, and wait for 5th Infantry Brigade to land at the end of May. But Northwood believed that Thompson's caution could lead to a political solution of both contestants occupying a patch of Falkland territory and when told more action was required, he returned to the Goose Green option and ordered Lieutenant-Colonel Hubert ('H') Jones, the 2 Para Commanding Officer, to attack Goose Green.

Jones was given his orders by Brigadier Thompson on 26 May on board *Fearless*. He then boarded *Intrepid* where the SAS suggested a company in defence. The Special Task Detachment, a Signals Intelligence unit, suggested the enemy strength of about 1,500 infantry, paras and commandos and that a clash would be equivalent of 2 Para as a Premier League football team playing a Sunday pub league team. Jones was in a hurry to return to 2 Para and met Captain Viv Rowe, the Brigade Intelligence Officer, on *Blue Beach* waiting to give him the most recent brigade intelligence. This came from several sources, including prisoners and documents captured at Port San Carlos, and confirmed that Task Force *Mercedes* was the equivalent of an infantry battle group supported by three 105mm Pack Howitzers and air defence artillery, a total strength of about 1,000 all ranks. However, Jones interrupted that he had just been told that the enemy was probably no more than a company and left Rowe to brief a captain with him. That night, 2 Para descended Sussex Mountain and by early on the 27th, it was squeezed into the house and ten outbuildings of Camilla Creek House, about five miles north of Goose Green. When the Signals Platoon tuned into the 10 a.m. BBC World Service News and heard 'A parachute battalion is poised and ready to assault Darwin and Goose Green', there was immediate concern of a breach of operational security. In fact, events on Falklands had been mentioned on domestic BBC channels and in Parliament the previous day. Argentine commanders assessed the announcement to be disinformation on the grounds that no commander in their right mind would broadcast an attack. Nevertheless, Brigadier-General Parada, still trapped in Stanley, ordered Task Force *Mercedes* to extend its 10-mile defensive perimeter north to 19 miles, but without reinforcements.

Several incidents hindered Lieutenant-Colonel Jones issuing his orders during the morning. One of two RAF Harriers supporting 2 Para was shot down and there were concerns that if the pilot was captured, the operations could be compromised; he was rescued three days later. A patrol ambushed a requisitioned blue Land Rover sent to investigate the BBC report and captured an officer and three soldiers. However, 2 Para had not taken a tactical interrogation team. It was not until about mid-afternoon that Jones issued his orders for a six-phase 4-mile advance with the aim of capturing Goose Green by first light next day. However, he was impatient and curtailed the briefing of his Intelligence Officer and concluded that 'All previous evidence suggests that if the enemy is hit hard, he will crumble.' No such evidence existed. The Blues and Royals and their tracked Scorpions and Scimitars were excluded from the order of battle because it was thought they could not negotiate the terrain.

Meanwhile, the rest of 3 Commando Brigade broke out of the San Carlos Water beachhead. 45 Commando 'yomped' ('your own marching pace') to Douglas and 3 Para 'tabbed' (tactical approach to battle) to Teal Inlet, which had been identified as the forward brigade logistic base. 40 Commando remained defending the beachhead. 42 Commando replaced 2 Para on Sussex Mountain. D Squadron was to reconnoitre Mount Kent.

As night fell on 27 May, 2 Para advanced from Camilla Creek House across the thick tussock grass covering flat ground and soon clashed with the enemy. By next morning, the battalion was held up north of Darwin Ridge. A company on the left flank faced considerable Argentine resistance and Lieutenant-Colonel Jones was killed making a lone assault on Darwin Hill that earned him the Victoria Cross. Major Chris Keeble, the Battalion Second-in-Command, assumed command and, ordering A Company to go firm, switched the weight of the attack to the right. B Company breached the defence at Boca House and was followed by D Company swinging left across the airstrip towards the school. Near the airstrip flag, 12 Platoon saw a white flag being waved from an enemy position and Lieutenant Jim Barry, the Platoon Commander, met with an Argentine officer. Both thought they were surrendering and when it became clear that no one was, Barry and his escort were returning to their position, still under a flag of truce, when they came under fire, controversially, from a British machine-gunner in the Darwin Ridge area presumably seeing 'enemy' in the open. The Argentines retaliated and Barry and two paras with him were killed. In the late afternoon, Argentine reinforcements from the Air Mobile Reserve (Combat Team *Solari*) on Mount Kent and First-Lieutenant Estaben and Combat Team *Guemes* in an Air Force Chinook and six Iroquois were escorted by a Puma gunship and six Hirundo A-109 gunships to a landing zone about 1,000 metres south of Goose Green. B Company organised shelling of the landing zone, just as the helicopters departed. While welcome, the reinforcement arrived too late to influence the battle.

Mr and Mrs Goss had watched the battle first from their bedroom window, then the sitting room and finally an underground shelter. In the Community Hall, 'Old Nan' McCallum was shielded by two freezers containing frozen meats and mattresses and blankets. Several tired and frightened conscripts had been denied shelter. In the late afternoon, Goss answered a knock on his front door to three battle-weary Argentine officers requesting that he and Willie Bowles accompany them to the Argentine HQ in Bailey's house. In the dining room, Wing-Commander Pedrozo told Goss he wanted to evacuate civilians and asked if he could help contact the British as he had only the international distress flares on the *Monsunen* tied up at the jetty. Shouting was pointless. Goss suggested his R/T radio, 'This is Eric Goss calling from Goose Green. Is anyone there?' To his surprise, Alan Miller at Port San Carlos answered and when Goss said he had foreign 'brass' who wished to contact the British, Miller asked 'Do you have many little men in green uniforms?' Goss responded, 'In excess of 1,000'. When Miller passed the message to HQ 3 Commando Brigade, Brigadier Thompson instructed Major Keeble to manage the ceasefire and suggested that two captured Argentine senior NCOs take the ultimatum to Piaggi, under a white flag. If they returned by 8.30 a.m. next day, surrender would be accepted; if not, let battle recommence.

The Argentine Army code of conduct permitted surrender when 50 per cent of the force are casualties and 75 per cent of the ammunition has been spent. Although this principle did not apply to Task Force *Mercedes*, Governor Menendez accepted it was trapped with no chance of reinforcement and on 29 May, Argentine Army Day and four days after (1810) Revolution Day, the two Argentines returned at 7 a.m. As the Argentine delegation left for the surrender negotiations at the airstrip hut, Goss handed Pedrozo a note written on *Amateur Radio* logbook paper he later shared with his officers,

> With your concern you show for the safety of civilians, can I now ask you to take this a step further and in view of the brave and courageous way your soldiers fought; in the interest of saving lives of such valiant soldiers on both sides – will you consider an honourable surrender? Britain and Argentina need these young men?

The Battle of Goose Green was a hard-won victory. Task Force *Mercedes* had shown resolve and of the about 800 Army and 200 Air Force before the battle, forty-seven Army were killed, ninety-eight were wounded and 1,000 were captured. Eighteen paras, one Army Air Corps and one Royal Engineer with 2 Para were killed. Persistent claims that 'very little accurate intelligence was received' is not reflected in the intelligence provided by HQ 3 Commando Brigade before and during the battle. That others were less informed is another issue. Clearing battlefields is always dangerous. Two days after the battle, three prisoners were killed and eight wounded when unstable ammunition exploded. An inquiry concluded that a British soldier shooting a gravely wounded Argentine in exploding ammunition was a humane act.

The treatment of the sick and wounded is governed by the First Geneva Convention. The British medical system, like most, escalates from self-treatment and colleagues to unit medical arrangements to field hospitals and general hospital. The Commando Logistic Regiment Medical Squadron and 5th Brigade's 16th Field Ambulance, Royal Army Medical Corps, both with Advanced Dressing Stations, were supported by the Main Dressing Station at Ajax Bay, which was nicknamed the 'Red and Green Life Giving Machine' and commanded by the charismatic Surgeon-Captain Rick Jolly. The quicker the evacuation, the greater chances of recovery.

Argentina was deeply suspicious of the ICRC and would only communicate with the British through Brazil. Indeed it was not until 6 June, a week before the end of the war, that triparte discussions took place between British, Argentina and the ICRC. Nevertheless, a maritime box in Grantham Sound, south of San Carlos Water, was agreed as a neutral zone so that ships displaying Red Cross insignia could collect the wounded. However, Argentina had converted naval transports previously used during the seizure of South Georgia and these were searched by the Royal Navy.

The Task Force included one hospital ship and three survey vessels, HMS *Hecla*, *Herald* and *Hydra*, converted to ambulance ships that transferred stabilised casualties to Montevideo or Ascension for casualty evacuation flights to RAF Brize Norton and a Service hospital. The P&O liner SS *Uganda* had been visiting Alexandria, Egypt, on a children's educational cruise when she was mobilised and disembarked her passengers at Naples on 10 April. Refitted as a 600-bed Her Majesty's Hospital Ship by the Gibraltar Dockyard, an innovation was fitting of the stern flight deck that enabled the wounded to be transferred by helicopter direct from the battlefield to theatre. The First Geneva Convention instructs that hospital ships must be 'brightly illuminated from dusk to dawn'. However, when the *Uganda* arrived in early May, she was initially an unwelcome beacon but quickly proved her worth. Casualties included battlefield wounds, burns, cold water immersion and weather and accidental injuries. Patients recovered in the Promenade Deck wards and were transferred to dormitory areas on a lower deck when fit enough.

Another innovation was the drafting of forty Senior and Junior Ratings of Queen Alexandra's Royal Naval Nursing Service from the naval hospitals at Haslar (Hampshire) and Stonehouse (Plymouth). They joined *Uganda* at Gibraltar on 16 April. For the first time, female Junior Ratings were permitted in an operational zone. There was also a Royal Navy psychiatrist and Anglican and Roman Catholic padres providing spiritual and welfare support. The Commando Forces Band helped transfer the wounded. Casualties included from HMS *Sheffield*, the intelligence trawler *Narwhal* and the bombings at Port Pleasant on 8 June. Three soldiers died of their wounds and about forty were single or double-limbed amputees.

As part of the Psychological Operations strategy, in early June, Captain Rod Bell, a Royal Marine born in Costa Rica and serving with HQ 3 Commando Brigade, broadcast a message after Doctor's Hour inviting Navy Captain Hussey to discuss a ceasefire. Dr Alison Bleaney, the acting Chief Medical Officer, thought Bell's accent so fluent, it must be a practical joke. Bell assured Hussey that Falklands Military Garrison was trapped and civilian casualties would be blamed on Argentina. Hussey, however, had no authority to negotiate but agreed daily contact at 1 p.m.; but there was no further contact, even after Bell had offered to evacuate casualties.

In late May, 11 Field Squadron, which was part of 38 Engineer Regiment and specialised in airfield construction, landed from LSL *Sir Bedivere* with orders to increase Harrier mission time by constructing an Aircraft Forward Operating Base near *Green Beach*. Although Prefabricated Surfacing Airfield Panels had been lost on the *Atlantic Conveyor*, enough replacement material was found on the *Sir Lancelot* to allow the squadron to lay a 260-metre runway on a slope, a vertical landing pad and four dispersal areas. 59 Independent Commando Squadron installed the Expeditionary Bulk Fuel Handling pumps but they were slow. 63 Squadron, RAF Regiment equipped with Rapier surface-to-air missiles, provided air defence. Alan Miller and farmers at Port San Carlos used their tractors to move equipment. The RAF knew the airstrip as 'RAF West Wittering', to the Royal Navy it was HMS *Sheathbill* and to the Army, it was 'Syd's Strip' in recognition of Squadron-Leader 'Syd' Morris' appointment as 'airport manager'. Helicopters were using the strip by 2 June and a pair of Royal Navy Sea Harriers were first to land three days later. It later emerged that Argentine pilots attacking San Carlos Water were flying so low, they did not see it.

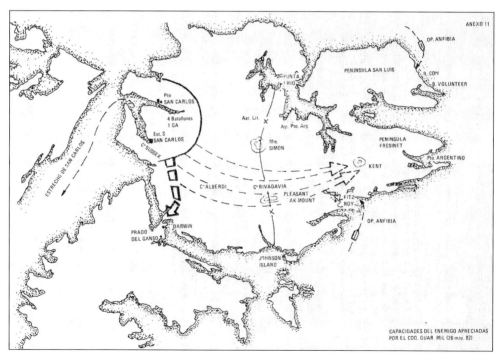

MAP L. Argentine Intelligence assessment dated 26 May suggested the British would break-out from San Carlos Water and would advance to Stanley using the southern route via Goose Green and Bluff Cove.

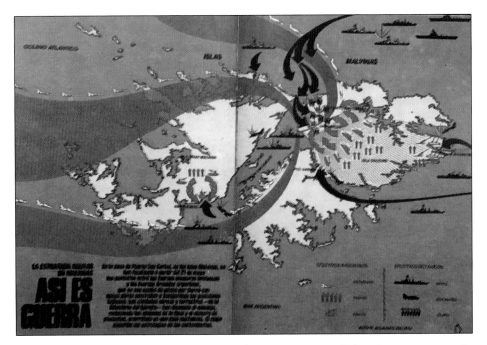

MAP M. Propaganda for public consumption showing Argentine all-directions counter-attacks on the San Carlos Water beachhead.

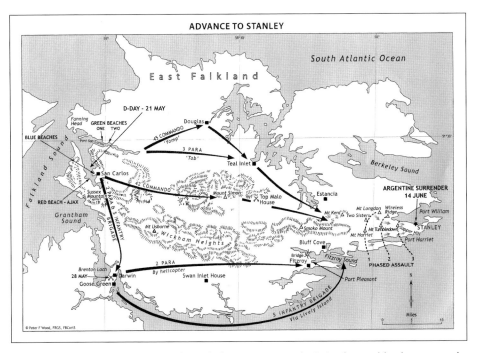

MAP N. Major-General Moore planned that 3 Commando Brigade would advance on the northern flank using Teal Inlet as a Forward Operating Base. 5th Infantry Brigade was to advance on the southern flank either by sea or land from Goose Green toward Bluff Cove. (Peter Wood)

29 May. After the Battle of Goose Green the previous day, Wing-Commander Wilson Pedrozo, the Argentine commander, is 'welcomed' to San Carlos by Brigadier Thompson. (Crown Copyright)

29 May. 'Gentlemen of the Press' attached to 3 Commando Brigade leave San Carlos for the 'yomp' to Stanley. Some journalists were expecting to be flown, however the loss of the *Atlantic Conveyor* meant supplies were a higher priority.

Goose Green prisoners. 'PW' (prisoner of war) and 'PG' ('prisionero de guerre') in English and Spanish respectively. The tubes are empty shell cases.

Goose Green. An Intelligence Corps Staff Sergeant examines captured Argentine documents. Interrogations also produced useful results.

The Breakout.
45 Commando took the advice of Alan Miller at Port San Carlos of reducing the 'yomp' (your own marching pace) to Douglas by using Rigid Raider Craft along the San Carlos River and 'yomp' across moorland to Teal Inlet. There was very little cover.

San Carlos. Land Rovers use the exit route from the two *Blue Beaches* en route to Teal Inlet. 4th Assault Squadron RM Armoured Recovery Vehicle is on the beach.

HQ 3 Commando Brigade underneath camouflage nets and digging in at Teal Inlet. (Crown Copyright)

Royal Marines bunker at Teal Inlet.

Three members of the Argentine Advanced Observer Post Mike-5 captured on 30 May at Top Malo House after being flown to San Carlos. Another post had been captured at Goose Green. The third reached Stanley. A Royal Navy medic is in attendance.

Forward Operating Base ('Sid's Strip') at Port San Carlos.

*Above*: The wreckage of the RAF GR3 Harrier that crashed on the strip. Note the message.

*Right*: A Sea Harrier low on fuel is diverted to HMS *Fearless*.

*Above*: The Sea Harrier on the *Fearless* Flight Deck.

*Left*: Royal Engineers repair the damage to 'Sid's Strip'.

The burning *Sir Galalad* at Fitzroy. Rafts are alongside the ship. (Chris Baxter)

Two Sisters. Low level air photograph showing an Argentine Blowpipe gunner and a tent. (Crown Copyright)

An Argentine 105 mm Pack Howitzer gun position on Stanley Common.

13 June. Mount Harriet. A 42 Commando sergeant and an Argentine medical officer treat a wounded conscript.

A Wessex collects wounded soldiers after the 3 Commando Brigade attack on the Outer Defence Zone.

A Blues and Royals Troop on the track to Stanley.

3 Commando Brigade preparing to move after the air raid during 12 June when four A-4Bs Skyhawks made seven passes, dropping bombs and machine-gunning the position.

14 June. The Artillery BV 202 had hit a mine during the night as HQ 3 Commando Brigade was moving after being bombed.

*Above left*: 14 June. HQ 3 Commando Brigade position on Two Sisters. Frequent snow squalls raced in from the southern ocean. (Author)

*Above right*: On 14 June, Privates Sergio Grabchuch (right) and Hector Mino sitting on the sea wall are focused on reading a letter from home. (Eduardo Rotondo)

*Left*: As 45 Commando advanced to Sapper Hill through minefields, Petty Officer Peter Holdgate, a Navy photographer, took this iconic photograph of Corporal Peter Robinson carrying a Union Jack to avoid 'friendly fire'. (Crown Copyright)

*Below*: In 1982, the Calvi Report into the Argentine performance shows that Tumbledown has been lost and the defence of Stanley rested on the Sapper Hill. The map is part of an order purchased by Argentina before the war (1:50,000 scale).

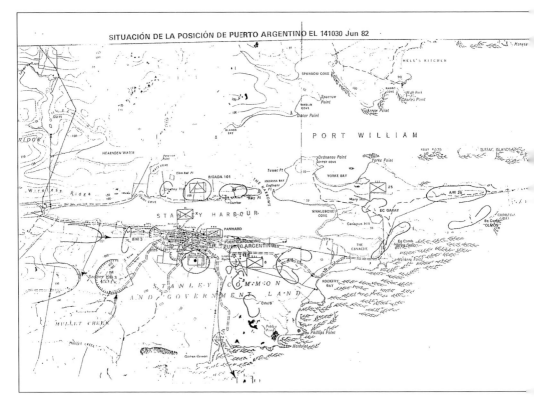

In the late afternoon, defeated Argentine troops retreat along Ross Street. In the background is the Town Hall.

14 June. Mid-afternoon. Brigadier Thompson and his Tactical HQ on the outskirts of Stanley listen to a radio message from General Moore that the Argentines were seeking a ceasefire. Left to right: Max Hastings lighting a cigar; Royal Military Police Cpl 'Dixie' Dean (Bodyguard); Cpl Robinson (radio operator); Brigadier Thompson, Major Rod MacDonald (59 Indep Cdo Squadron Royal Engineers); Lt Col Mike Holroyd-Smith (29 Cdo Regt); and Marine 'Geordie' McGuire. Shortly after this photograph was taken, Hastings asked to go to Stanley.

Lieutenant-Colonel
Rose (in desert cap),
his radio operator
(in blue jacket)
and Captain Bell
are escorted to
the Secretariat by
Wing-Commander
Bloomer-Reeves.
(Eduardo Rotondo)

Headquarters, Land Forces
Falkland Islands

INSTRUMENT OF SURRENDER

I, the undersigned, Commander of all the Argentine land, sea and
air forces in the Falkland Islands *//3M* unconditionally surrender to Major
General J. J. MOORE CB OBE MC* as representative of Her Brittanic
Majesty's Government.

Under the terms of this surrender all Argentinian personnel in the
Falkland Islands are to muster at assembly points which will be nominated
by General Moore and hand over their arms, ammunition, and all other
weapons and warlike equipment as directed by General Moore or appropriate
British officers acting on his behalf.

Following the surrender all personnel of the Argentinian Forces
will be treated with honour in accordance with the conditions set out
in the Geneva Convention of 1949. They will obey any directions
concerning movement and in connection with accommodation.

This surrender is to be effective from *2359* hours ZULU on *14* June
(*2059* hours local) and includes those Argentine Forces presently
deployed in and around Port Stanley, those others on East Falkland,
*/M3M* West Falkland and all the outlying islands.

............................ Commander Argentine Forces

............................ J. J. MOORE
                             Major General

............................ Witness

*2359*
............................ hours *14* June 1982

A copy of the
formal Instrument of
Surrender signed by
Major-General Moore
and Brigadier-General
Menendez.

General Moore pencil drafted a signal on paper which was radioed by SAS Satcom operator to Hereford and then relayed to the Ministry of Defence in London, where Menendez's name was misspelt.

```
VZCZCBMA020     UU
OO RBDAPZ
DE RBDTWM 002 1660155
ZNR UUUUU
O 150120Z JUN 82
FM TPS HEREFORD
TO RBDEC/CTF 317
RBDFNT/CTG 317.8
RBDFNR/CTG 317.0
RBDICU/CTG 317.9
INFO RBDAPZ/CTU 317.1.1
RBDAPZ/CTU 317.1.2
BT
UNCLAS
SIC 19F
THE FOLLOWING IS THE TEXT OF A MSG FROM 317.1 PASSED VIA HEREFORD TO
ADDRESSEES ABOVE.  MSG BEGINS.
HQ LFFI PORT STANLEY.  IN PORT STANLEY AT 9 O'CLOCK PM FALKLAND
ISLANDS TIME TONIGHT THE 14 JUNE 1982, MAJOR GENERAL MENENDES
SURRENDERED TO ME ALL THE ARGENTINE ARMED FORCES IN EAST AND WEST
FALKLAND, TOGETHER WITH THEIR IMPEDIMENTA.    ARRANGEMENTS ARE IN
HAND TO ASSEMBLE THE MEN FOR RETURN TO ARGENTINA, TO GATHER IN
THEIR ARMS AND EQUIPMENT, AND TO MARK AND MAKE SAFE THEIR MUNITIONS.
THE FALKLAND ISLANDS ARE ONCE MORE UNDER THE GOVERNMENT DESIRED


PAGE 2 RBDTWM 002 UNCLAS
BY THEIR INHABITANTS.
GOD SAVE THE QUEEN.
SIGNED JJ MOORE.
MSG ENDS
BT
```

*Above left*: Max Hastings claims to be the first to 'enter' Stanley. (Eduardo Rotondo)

*Above right*: 15 June. Naval Party 8901, (J Company, 42 Commando) captured in April, raise the Union flag at Government House.

# Chapter 9

# The Advance to Stanley –
# 1 to 10 June

After a flight from RAF Brize Norton to Ascension, Major-General Moore and Brigadier Tony Wilson and their headquarters embarked on the *Queen Elizabeth Two*. During the leg to South Georgia, a modern satellite communication system installed on the ship failed, isolating Moore except for the BBC World Service. At South Georgia, they and their key staff cross-decked to HMS *Antrim* and landed at *Blue Beach* on 29 May.

Since there were no indications that Army Group Stanley was deploying from its fortress, Moore confirmed his plan for the assault:

Phase One – 11/12 June
3 Commando Brigade. Assault Outer Defence Zone.
 3 Para – Mount Longdon.
 45 Commando – Two Sisters.
 42 Commando – Mount Harriet.

Phase Two – 12/13 June
Both Brigades. Seize the southern sector of the Inner Defence Zone.
 Scots Guards – Mount Tumbledown.
 2 Para – Wireless Ridge.

Phase Three – 13/14 June
5th Infantry Brigade. Seize remainder of Inner Defence Zone.
 1/7th Gurkha Rifles – Capture Mount William.
 1 Welsh Guards – Capture Sapper Hill

Phase Four – 14 June
3 Commando Brigade covered by 5th Infantry Brigade. Break into Stanley. Fighting in the town predicted.

The Blues and Royals provided a troop to both brigades. The two Argentine Armoured Cavalry Reconnaissance Squadrons, equipped with Panhard AML-90s, were known to be defending Stanley. It was not then known that 181 Squadron was dismounted.

## 3 COMMANDO BRIGADE – NORTHERN FLANK

As the Commando Brigade broke out from the San Carlos Water beachhead and headed east, the recently formed Argentine 602 Commando Company laid a tripwire of three patrols north–south across East Falkland. But one patrol clashed with the SAS on Mount Kent (1.099 feet/333 metres) and another was destroyed by the Mountain and Arctic Warfare Cadre, Royal Marines, at Top Malo House on 31 May, capturing five prisoners. The third patrol on Wickham Heights overlooked the southern coast.

Throughout the advance, the Falklanders gave invaluable support. Shortly before 3 Para departed from Port San Carlos, Terry Peck arrived on 31 May and was debriefed by Brigade Intelligence; he proved to be a reliable source of recent information in Stanley and the North Camp district of East Falkland. D (Patrol) Company invited him to be a scout. Teal Inlet and its jetty had been designated as the brigade forward echelon for helicopters flying supplies to the brigade, but the loss of helicopters was having an impact. At Estancia. Peck noted 3 Para was struggling to move ammunition and supplies to the companies preparing to assault Mount Longdon and suggested to Major Roger Patton, the Battalion Quartermaster, that local farmers be invited to help with their vehicles and driving expertise. Within about twelve hours, Mrs Trudi Morrison (now Trudi McPhee) of Green Patch had assembled a 'wagon train' of tractors and cross-country vehicles and co-drivers riding 'shotgun' from several farms. Her father was John Pole-Evans, the radio amateur and owner of the blue Land Rover captured at Goose Green. As common among those serving, the volunteers wrote a last letter to relatives in case they were killed or died. One commented that 'Writing that message to my parents was the hardest thing of the whole war.

Major Patten briefed Trudi each morning of the requirements and she then tasked drivers, some collecting consignments from Teal inlet, a six-hour return journey, and others delivering supplies to the company echelons. Bruce May, from Johnson Harbour, remembered being told to abandon his vehicle if attacked by aircraft. After an afternoon of rest, convoys usually formed up at 4.30 p.m. Headlight bulbs had been removed and military clothing was worn to prevent snipers identifying the activity. To help with some cross-country night navigation, Trudi walked in front of the lead vehicle wearing large white gloves behind her back, indicating direction 'Straight on' (hands behind her back) and indicating turn left or centre. Vehicles inevitably bogged, however local knowledge and cross-country skills proved invaluable with Patrick Minto and his brother, Ally, winning a worthy reputation. Shortly before Battle of Mount Longdon, Major Patten asked Trudi to mark out a helicopter landing site for casualty evacuation. For Neil Rowlands, aged sixteen, and driving a tractor, seeing the wounded was something he would never forget. Miss McPhee was later awarded a Commendation for Bravery from Admiral Fieldhouse. A group arrived from Long Island armed with the rifles cached by Corporal York and his NP 8901 section in April.

A 45 Commando patrol patrolling Mount Kent found the Air Mobile Reserve Command Post (Combat Team *Solari*) and collected substantial intelligence in an abandoned cave passed to HQ 3 Commando Brigade. The deployment to Goose Green had clearly been rushed. Priceless Document Intelligence included the Strategic Reserve Operation Order for the helicopter 601 Combat Aviation Battalion, a map showed regimental deployments and a list of unit strengths of Army Group Stanley giving a total of 7,176 all ranks. The document again proved the accuracy of 3 Commando Brigade Intelligence, which had allowed an estimated 10,000 all ranks trapped in Stanley. An estimated 2,000 were trapped on West Falkland.

3 Commando Brigade had spent nearly seven weeks on ships and had been ashore for three weeks. The weather was becoming increasingly hostile, winter was creeping from high ground and a bright moon cast long shadows across the moorland. By 8 June, Brigadier Thompson was ready to attack.

## 5TH INFANTRY BRIGADE – SOUTHERN FLANK

Brigadier Wilson had exploited every opportunity to advance to the Bluff Cove/Fitzroy sector and be ready to assault Stanley. A Brigade HQ attempt to drive the 35 miles in Land Rovers using a muddy track proved impassible. And then a 2 Para patrol reached Swan House and, telephoning to Fitzroy, found out there were no Argentines. The battalion reacted quickly and about eighty men, including a mortar detachment and Tactical HQ, squeezed into the surviving Chinook and six 656 Squadron Scout helicopters and seized Fitzroy. The Argentines also had Chinooks and when a Royal Marines Mountain & Arctic Warfare patrol on Wickham Heights watching the southern coast saw the helicopter, assumed it to be Argentine and tasked 7 Commando Battery on Mount Kent with a fire mission – until a break in the clouds identified *Bravo November*.

Next day, the remainder of 2 Para arrived, including the new Commanding Officer, Lieutenant-Colonel David Chaundler. He had joined the Task Force after parachuting into the South Atlantic. On 4 June, the Brigade Signals Squadron improved communications by inserting a signals rebroadcast detachment on Pleasant Peak on Wickham Heights midway Goose Green and Bluff Cove. The Heights were also used by Argentine aircraft as a route to Stanley Airport. Enthusiasm by Brigade HQ to advance to Bluff Cove was hampered by inexperience in maritime operations and endless changes of plans. No sooner had Amphibious Warfare devised a plan to move the two Guards battalions to Bluff Cove using *Fearless* and *Intrepid* when Northwood declared that since two landing ships would be within range of land-based Exocets in Stanley their political weight was graded to equate to aircraft-carriers and not to be risked. Eventually, Major Ewen Southby-Tailyour, a Royal Marine with expert knowledge of the Falklands gained while sailing around the coast and in amphibious operations, co-ordinated the deployment.

In Phase One during the night of 6 June, *Intrepid* ferried the Scots Guards and other units to Lively Island and then the troops cross-decked to her four open-decked LCUs for the 20-mile transfer to Fitzroy. Meanwhile, when the Pleasant Peak signals detachment reported a fault they could not resolve, Major Mike Forge and Staff Sergeant Joe Baker, both Brigade Signal Squadron, left San Carlos in a 656 Squadron Army Air

Corps Gazelle and flew at low level toward Pleasant Peak. The destroyer HMS *Cardiff* was on the Stanley gunline bombarding targets when her radar acquired an aircraft signature using the Heights and believing it to be Argentine, two Sea Dart missiles were fired at the acquisition. About two hours later, the destroyer withdrew from the gunline and was near Lively Island when four surface contacts were identified heading north. Already alerted by the previous contact, the destroyer fired starshell, which illuminated the landing craft and disappeared.

Southby-Tailyour guided the landing craft to Bluff Cove at dawn and although the troops were wet and cold, the Scots Guards took over from 2 Para. The paras had orders to withdraw to Fitzroy, but Fitzroy Bridge, about a mile west of Bluff Cove, was thought prepared for demolition. The alternative option was a 12-mile cross-country march around the head of Port Fitzroy and before he returned to Port San Carlos to organise Phase Two the next night, Southby-Tailyour agreed the LCUs could ferry 2 Para across the mouth of Bluff Cove Creek. He emphasised they must be at Bluff Cove on the next night. But after he left for San Carlos, an officer insisted the coxswains ferry the battalion across Port Fitzroy to Fitzroy where the LCUs became stormbound and out of position. Meanwhile, a patrol from the Rebroadcast detachment had found the wreckage of the Gazelle and all four on board dead.

In Phase Two the next night, *Fearless* departed from San Carlos Water with the Embarked Force that included the Welsh Guards, which had orders to land at Bluff Cove , and 1 Troop, 9 Parachute Squadron, Royal Engineers, who were tasked to repair Fitzroy Bridge. *Fearless* reached Elephant Island, about 8 miles north of Lively Island, but there was no sign of Southby-Tailyour and the landing craft. Captain Jeremy Larken, the *Fearless* Commanding Officer, therefore ordered half of the Welsh Guards and the para engineers to embark on two LCUs and instructed Major Tony Todd, a Royal Corps of Transport officer with maritime experience, to navigate them to Bluff Cove. *Fearless* returned to San Carlos Water and cross-decked the remainder of the Embarked Force to the LSL *Sir Galahad*. Other 5th Infantry Brigade assets had already departed on the LSL *Sir Tristram*; it was also carrying stores to repair Fitzroy Bridge. *Sir Galahad* arrived at Port Pleasant at about 8.30 a.m. One principle learnt by Commando Brigade from its experiences at San Carlos was to land troops quickly, but this was an unfamiliar principle within 5th Brigade and there were delays and misunderstandings, not the least of which was the Welsh Guards expecting to land at Bluff Cove.

While the Fleet Air Arm and RAF had the luxury of two aircraft-carriers and a forward operating base, the Argentine Air Force and Naval Air Command operated from Comodoro Rivadavia in northern Argentina (600 miles from Stanley), Rio Gallegos (480 miles) and Rio Grande (420 miles). Air Force Delta-wing Dassault Mirages and Israeli Daggers fighters flying combat speeds suffered from significant fuel consumption that reduced range. Part of mission planning was to ensure 1 Group KC-130 Hercules tankers were in the right place at the right height and time to refuel attacking aircraft returning to their bases. *Canberra* bombers and 35A Learjets provided photographic reconnaissance. The worst day was 21 May, D-Day, when eleven aircraft were shot down with the loss of three Air Force and one Navy pilot. So far, the Air Force 5th Fighter Group equipped with A-4B Skyhawks had damaged *Glasgow* shelling shore positions on 12 May, shared in sinking *Ardent* in Grantham Sound and damaged *Argonaut* on D-Day, sank *Antelope* on the 24th and *Coventry* the next day and damaged

*Broadsword* acting as a decoy north-west of Falkland Sound. The greatest losses were seven Air Force when a C-130 Electronic Reconnaissance Hercules was shot down and a Learjet was shot down on 7 June with the loss of five aircrew.

8 June dawned a bright day. Sea Harriers drove off three Mirages IIIs attacking San Carlos Water during the morning. The increased activity at Port Fitzroy had been from several sources, including the Advanced Observer Post on Mount Harriet using powerful binoculars. At about 1.15 a.m., a RAF Harrier suffered engine failure at 'Sid's Strip' while hovering and ripped up the metal runway as it careered towards a Rapier Firing Unit. A second Harrier landed on the wreckage of the runway and two 800 Squadron Sea Harriers, both low on fuel, hovered onto the HMS *Fearless* and HMS *Intrepid* flight decks respectively. During the early afternoon, HMS *Plymouth* was badly damaged in a Dagger attack. A 5th Group Skyhawk flight scouting the south coast of East Falkland spotted ships masts in Fitzroy Cove and attacked, hitting *Sir Galahad* and *Sir Tristram*, which were still loaded with troops waiting to land. As the Skyhawks withdrew along Choiseul Sound, they crippled a *Fearless* LCU en route to Bluff Cove carrying four HQ 5th Brigade Land Rovers fitted with radios. Total British casualties were fifty killed and fifty-seven wounded, some with burns requiring specialist treatment. When the *Uganda* entered Grantham Sound to embark the wounded, the ICRC rejected an Argentine protest that the ship was delivering military equipment.

The Argentine LADA office and Stanley Town Hall in 2018. In 1982, the LADA was the centre of Argentine intelligence operations before the war and was occupied by HQ 3 Commando Brigade Intelligence as a base. Radios, equipment and substantial information were found. (Author)

Stanley. The Stanley School on St John's Street, which had been an Argentine HQ, is searched for intelligence.

Stanley Public Jetty. Prisoners are screened at the Stanley Public Jetty before repatriation on the *Canberra*. In the lower right corner of the photo is an oil drum marked Malima for waste/refuse distributed by Argentine Civil Affairs early during the occupation.

*Left*: 17 June. Stanley Public Jetty. 160 (5th Infantry Brigade) Provost Company search prisoners.

*Below*: Stanley Public Jetty. Prisoners wait to board *Canberra*.

Fox Bay East. A 40 Commando Royal Marines escorts prisoners to be embarked on a ship for repatriation.

Captured AML Panhard armoured cars of the 10th Armoured Reconnaissance Squadron on Philomel Street. (Author)

Flooded 105 mm Pack Howitzer gun pit. (Author)

Prisoners load Argentine weapons into a lorry for disposal.

A land-based Exocet from the *Guerrica* modified by an officer captured at Stanley. On the last night, a missile damaged HMS *Glamorgan* and caused casualties as it was withdrawing from the gun-line. (Author)

Special Category officer prisoners held at the Ajax Bay prison camp.

A cartoon found during a search of prisoners at Ajax Bay. Translated as 'The Six of San Carlos'.

19 June. A convoy of ships approaching Stanley with reinforcements.

11 July. *Canberra* almost alongside her berth at Southampton to an unexpected welcome of families. Embarked on board was principally 3 Commando Brigade. (Author)

12 July, Port Madryn. During the day, Argentina surrendered and the prisoners on the roll-on/roll-off ferry *St Edmund* were released. In the photograph are Brigadier-General Menendez (Malvinas Governor), Brigadier-General Jofre (10th Brigade), Brigadier-General Parada (3rd Brigade) and Commander Robacio (5th Marines). The welcoming party include Marine Vice-Admiral Busser, planner of the 2 April invasion, and Vice-Admiral Lombardo (South Atlantic Theatre of Naval Operations), who planned Operation *Rosario*.

24 July 1982. Clearing the battlefields was dangerous. The Land Forces Falklands Islands Intelligence Section searches Mount Harriet for dead Argentines. Some were booby-trapped.

De-mining of the Falklands. (Safeline Global Ltd)

*Above*: Major Gerald Cheek commands the Falklands Islands Defence Force detachment on the 2019 Remembrance Day Service at Stanley Cathedral. As the Senior Service, the Royal Navy leads the march to the War Memorial and are followed by the Welsh Guards roulement infantry company and the RAF. (Crown Copyright)

*Right*: Eric Goss, Goose Green Farm Manager in 1982, at the Falkland Island Government office in London in mid-1997. During the 1991 royal visit to the Falkands, he hosted the visit by HRH the Duke of Edinburgh. (Eric Goss)

*Above*: Stanley, 2018. (Author)

*Left*: Port Stanley. The second *Lady Elizabeth* was launched in 1879 and delivered cargo. She was damaged in 1912 in a storm while sailing around Cape Horn and limped into Port Stanley. She later hit a rock at Volunteer Point and became a Falkland Islands Company floating warehouse until, in 1936, she broke free of her moorings in a storm and beached at Whalebone Cove, where she still remains.

# Chapter 10

# Capture of Stanley

The attack of Fitzroy forced Major-General Moore to schedule the assault on Stanley to 11 June. 5th Infantry Brigade concentrated at Bluff Cove and the Welsh Guards casualties were replaced by A and C Companies, 40 Commando and a 59 Independent Commando Squadron troop.

Concerned about the precarious nature of the defence of *Las Malvinas,* Governor Menendez and his senior commanders agreed next day that Brigadier-General Daher, his Deputy Commander, should return to Argentina and consult with President Galtieri. Civil Affairs meanwhile advised that the naval bombardment of Stanley Common was endangering civilians living east of the Battle Memorial, near Government House, and they should leave their houses. Indeed on 11 June, three women, Doreen Bonner, a third generation 'kelper, Mary Goodwin, a mother dedicated to her disabled daughter, and Susan Whitley, a teacher and recently married to Steve, the island vet, were killed by a 'rogue' shell fired from a British warship hitting the house in which they were sheltering. Some civilians placing bedsheets, some pink, on washing lines. Predicting fighting in Stanley, the ICRC mediated a neutral zone around the Anglican Cathedral, which led to a delegate commenting that the agreement was 'a rare occurrence in the history of international humanitarian law'.

During the night of 11/12 June, 3 Commando Brigade attacked the Outer Defence Zone in Phase One.

**Mount Longdon** (541 feet/165 metres)
Mount Longdon was on the left flank of the brigade attack and was defended by B Company, 7th Infantry Regiment, and two 5th Marines platoons occupying bunkers among rock runs. Among the reservists was James Craig. His grandfather had served in the Grenadier Guards during the First World War and had emigrated in 1923 and his father had served in the British Army during the Second World War and had also emigrated. After graduating from school in 1980, Craig played on a rugby tour to Britain and was conscripted in 1981. He did not want to fight, however his father told him 'We've never had a deserter in this family, and it's not going to happen now'. Craig

described life on Mount Longdon: 'We were cold, wet and hungry. Our clothes were completely inadequate for the conditions, we didn't even have an anorak at first. I had three pairs of socks which I wore all at once'.

3 Para planned to attack Mount Longdon directly from the west. In support was 79 Commando Battery. At the Start Line, about 800 metres west and below Longdon, Support Company briefly mingled with B Company in the area of Murrell Bridge. At 8.15 p.m., about fifteen minutes behind schedule, A Company seized the northerly spur. As B Company advanced toward the summit, a mine exploded and gritty fighting developed as the paras, taunted by Argentines in bunkers and shouting American gangster jargon, tackled rocky bunkers in 'Grenade Alley'. Sergeant Ian McKay was awarded a posthumous Victoria Cross for assaulting a bunker. A Company moved to the left of B Company and then the paras systematically infiltrated through the rocks, with paras marking enemy positions with cigarettes or torches.

By about 1.30 a.m., Major Carrizo-Salvadores, the defending commander, had lost direct communications with his platoon commanders and Regimental Headquarters on Wireless Ridge and was forced to relay messages through Army Group Stanley, which slowed the passage of information. He had no alternative but to withdraw to Wireless Ridge. Private Craig: 'We fought overnight and then at daylight when there was a pause in the fighting, most of the officers had gone.'

By daylight 3 Para had captured Mount Longdon and formed up to receive a counter-attack. The ten-hour battle cost 3 Para seventeen killed, mostly B Company. However, shelling over the next two days cost four killed and ten wounded. Of the 287 defenders, thirty-one were killed, about 120 were wounded and fifty were captured.

**Two Sisters**
The twin peaks of Two Sisters (919 feet/280 metres) was in the centre of the brigade attack. A and C Companies, 4th Infantry Regiment, and B Company, 8th Infantry Regiment, were in defence. 45 Commando planned a three-phase assault supported by 8 Commando Battery, HMS *Glamorgan* and the 40 Commando Milan Troop converted to heavy weapons.

In the first phase X Company and Milan Troop ,carrying the heavy firing posts and missiles, found the 6 kilometre route surveyed by Recce Troop from Mt Wall difficult and reached their Start Line two and half hours behind schedule. Lieutenant-Colonel Andrew Whitehead, the Commanding Officer, calmly advised he would order the advance when all was ready. Ten minutes later, X Company advanced and was within 600 metres of Two Sisters (West) when it was pinned down for the next three hours by Argentines in rocky bunkers. 8 Commando Battery was tasked on other missions and the Mortar Troop 81 mm mortars recoiled into the soft turf. To the north in the second phase, Y and Z Companies crossed the Murrell Bridge and were advancing near direct south towards Two Sisters (East) when a flare exposed the Royal Marines on the tussock-covered slopes to shelling and mortars. Casualties were taken. Lieutenant Clive Dytor, commanding 8 Troop, realised there were two options – withdraw or advance – and in an inspirational example of leadership, he ordered 'Forward, everybody!' With Z Company shouting its battle cry 'Zulu, Zulu', both companies surged up the slope and overran the Argentine positions. Some enemy withdrew to 5th Marines on Mount Tumbledown while others joined the defence of Stanley. X Company went firm on Two Sisters (West).

The battle had lasted about two and a half hours and cost British forces three Royal Marines and a Royal Engineer. Twenty Argentines were killed, fifty wounded and fifty-four taken prisoner. Lieutenant-Colonel Whitehead later commented, 'If we had a Company up here, we would have died of old age before it was captured'. Lieutenant Dytor was awarded the Military Cross. Within two hours, 45 Commando was ready to exploit to Mount Tumbledown.

## Mount Harriet (873 feet/288 metres)

Defending the south-west sector of Army Group Stanley were two 4th Infantry Regiment companies on the right flank of the brigade attack. The sister regiment, 12th Infantry Regiment, had surrendered at Goose Green.

After ten days of plotting minefields, Lieutenant-Colonel Nick Vaux, the 42 Commando Officer, planned a diversion to support the main attack from the south-east. 7 Commando Battery was in support.

After dark, K and L Companies and 'Porter' Troop carrying GPMGs and 10,000 rounds of ammunition negotiated the minefield to the south-west of Mount Harriet and, passing around a small lake, headed towards the forming-up place near a track junction about 700 metres south of Mount Harriet. The Welsh Guards platoon securing the Start Line was repositioned and two Milan anti-tank posts guarded approaches from Stanley.

As 7 Battery started shelling the ridge, 12 Troop, mainly former NP 8901 captured in April, and J Company simulated a patrol clash and drew fire from Mount Harriet. K Company climbed the southern slopes, turned right at the top and attacked the defence. The Argentine 3rd Artillery Group near Stanley used the burning Command Post as a marker. L Company followed K Company and, turning left at the top, overran the western defences. 5 Troop then advanced across 800 metres of open ground towards Goat Ridge (305 feet/93 metres) in between Mount Harriet and Two Sisters but drew fire and withdrew. The Troop and 4 Troop then combined to capture the objective. As the wreckage of 4th Regiment withdrew from Mount Harriet, the diversion negotiated a large minefield and 42 Commando expected a counter-attack from Tumbledown; it did not materialise. The Argentines lost nine killed, fifty-three wounded and over 300 captured, including the Commanding Officer, against three Royal Marines killed and twenty-eight wounded. By dawn, snow was joining smoke drifting across the battlefield.

As HMS *Glamorgan* and *Yarmouth* withdrew from the gunline 17 miles to the south of Stanley shortly before dawn. *Glamorgan* clipped the shore-based Exocet zone and lost nine men killed and fourteen wounded, mostly chefs and helicopter maintenance crews from a missile.

3 Commando Brigade had captured the Outer Defence Zone and had reduced 7th Regiment to two companies and destroyed 4th Regiment and was expecting 5th Infantry Brigade to attack in Phase Two. But with some justification, Brigadier Wilson was not keen to assault the Inner Defence Zone without reconnaissance and

successfully lobbied Major-General Moore for a twenty-four-hour delay. His artillery also needed resupply. As the mist cleared to a sunny day, Argentine artillery shelled the three captured ridges and among the casualties was Corporal Denzil Connick of 3 Para, who was severely wounded. He would be instrumental in forming the South Atlantic Medal Association. In the mid-afternoon, a flight of four 5th Fighter Group A-4 Skyhawks bombed and machine-gunned HQ 3 Commando Brigade, forcing a 'crash' night move and transfer of command to Brigade Tactical HQ. As the column crossed the Murrell River, the overloaded Intelligence Section BV 202 capsized in the river. As the column then headed through Louis Pass to the hills overlooking the battlefield, the Artillery BV ran over a mine and a Royal Artillery officer was seriously wounded and could not be evacuated until daylight. The driver kept him warm from the bitterly cold wind and snow. The column also had to extract itself from the mines. Command was returned at dawn.

## PHASE TWO – 13/14 JUNE.

### Mount Tumbledown (748 feet/228 metres)
Brigadier Wilson planned the Scots Guards would seize Mount Tumbledown followed by the Gurkhas attacking Mount William and then both would be in position to support the Welsh Guards attack on Sapper Hill.

Defending Tumbledown was the 5th Marine Infantry Battalion in a 12-mile perimeter. It also defended Mount William (696 feet/213 metres), about 700 metres to the south, and Two Sisters, 5,000 metres to the east. Under command was C Company, 6th Infantry Regiment, to west of Sapper Hill. In direct support was a marine artillery battery. On its right flank in depth was A Company, 3rd Infantry Regiment, south of Moody Brook.

Early on 13 June, Sea Kings lifted the Scots Guards from Bluff Cove to Goat Ridge. In his first phase, Lieutenant-Colonel Scott planned to use the track from Pony Pass, south of Mount William, to Stanley for a diversion. The three Guards companies were each allocated about a third of Tumbledown and 'Hey, Jimmy' was adopted as a password because Argentines had difficulty pronouncing the letter 'J' in English. Berets were worn to help identification from the helmeted Argentines. 1/7th Gurkhas were ready to attack Mount William in Phase Three, ideally by dawn.

The diversion of twelve Scots Guards, a Blues and Royals troop, two 9 Para Squadron RE and a mortar fire controller ran into a minefield south of Mount William and a Scorpion was damaged. On Tumbledown, the second phase, G Company led the advance up the lower slopes of Tumbledown and at about 2.30 a.m. handed the third phase to Left Flank, which soon ran into stubborn a defence from marines, marine engineers and a 4th Regiment platoon that had fought on Mount Harriet. Left Flank reached the heights but such were the demands of clearing positions of enemy, treating casualties and guarding prisoners meant that just seven reached the top; three were quickly wounded by machine-gun fire. 5th Marines were denied permission to counter-attack. Right Flank completed the capture of Tumbledown. Six Scots Guards were killed and thirty-five wounded. Argentine casualties were an estimated thirty killed, 100 wounded and thirty captured.

Meanwhile, the Welsh Guards advancing from Bluff Cove were on the Pony Pass track and ran into the same minefield south of Mount Harriet encountered by the Scots Guards diversion. As the Commando Engineer Troop moved to the front of the column, 400 Guardsmen and Royal Marines were reluctant to move off the track. After about an hour, 9 Troop, 40 Commando, at the head of the column, noticed several Royal Engineers were sitting down and assuming they had breached the minefield, bade them a cheerful 'Thanks, lads' unaware that sappers had not finished. The diversion and the mines detonating led to 5th Marines moving a company onto the track. By dawn, snow and smoke drifted across the battlefield.

## Mount William (325 feet/99 metres)

Mount William was defended by a marine infantry company and C Company, 3rd Infantry Regiment, in depth on the track south of Sapper Hill.

1/7th Gurkhas needed to be in position ready to assault Mount William by dawn. However, when the Scots Guards rejected their offer of reinforcements, the battalion ignored the fighting on Tumbledown and following a sheep path below the northern cliffs, breached two minefields, and then heading south passed behind the Scots Guards, had captured Mount William by dawn and formed up to support the attack on Sapper Hill.

## Sapper Hill

Meanwhile, the Welsh Guards were forming up to assault Sapper Hill, however, Navy pilots inexperienced in map reading mistakenly landed A (Welsh Guards) Company and 9 Troop, C Company, 40 Commando, on the track below the Argentine position. In a short battle, two Royal Marines were wounded and three Argentine marines were killed. A Combat Engineer Tractor and a half-section of 9 Para RE then clattered onto the hill having driven all the way from Fitzroy and was followed by a 4th Troop Blues and Royals Scimitar leading the Welsh Guards to the top of Sapper Hill. Half an hour later, 45 Commando arrived having previously being tasked by 3 Commando Brigade to capture the feature.

## Wireless Ridge (233 feet/68 metres)

2 Para, under command of 3 Commando Brigade, had advanced from Mount Longdon with orders to capture Wireless Ridge, known by the Argentines as *Cordon de la Radio*, north of Moody Brook. The ridge was defended largely by the 10th Armoured Recconnaisance Squadron and elements of 7th Infantry Regiment.

In a classic 'fire and movement' tactic, D Company captured the low feature *Rough Diamond* as a firebase. In the second phase, B Company in the centre and A Company on the left, supported by 3rd Troop, Blues and Royals, seized the spur Apple Pie overlooking Wireless Ridge to the south. In the third phase, D Company advanced south and then seized the eastern peak of Wireless Ridge, nicknamed 'Blueberry Hill', and defeated a listless counter-attack from Moody Brook Barracks. In the fourth phase overlooking the Murrell River, C (Patrol) Company captured *Northern Spur* and Ring Tour 100 to dominate Hearnden Water and threats from the east, the garrison at Cortley Ridge. B Company moved south and established a block on the western slopes of Tumbledown.

## Cortley Ridge

Meanwhile, 17 (Boat Troop) SAS and several SBS planned to use the fighting on Wireless Ridge by raiding the oil storage facilities on Cortley Ridge. It was known to be strongly defended by a 30 mm air defence battery and a 3rd Marine Battalion platoon. The 1st Raiding Squadron Royal Marines supplied Rigid Raider assault boats. As the force approached the mouth of the Murrell River, a National Border Guard Special Forces officer on the *Almirante Irizar* hospital ship in Port William spotted them. The defenders were already fully alerted to the fighting on Wireless Ridge and opened heavy fire on the raid, forcing them to withdraw at the cost of a Rigid Raider sinking close to the beach.

# Chapter 11

# Surrender of Argentine Ambitions in the South Atlantic

By the late afternoon, Army Group Stanley had given up the fight. As Argentina faced defeat, political rivalries surfaced, particularly in the Army where many officers were politically hostile to President Galtieri.

General Moore wanted to avoid fighting in a built-up area and ordered to 3 Commando Brigade to pursue Army Group Stanley. 5th Infantry Brigade and the ships offshore provided cover. 3rd Troop, Blues and Royals and 2 Para captured Moody Brook and advanced on the heels of the enemy retreating to Stanley. Brigadier Thompson and his Tactical HQ were following and then his radio operator reported he could not contact 2 Para. The general opinion was either the Battalion Command Post radio batteries had packed up, or, more likely, their radio to Brigade HQ was switched off. Thompson then met HQ 29 Commando Regiment on the outskirts of Stanley and 2 Para was instructed to halt. 'Roger' came the reply.

When reports emerged a ceasefire had been negotiated between London and Buenos Aries, Major-General Moore ordered 'weapons tight' and no units were to cross the limit of exploitation near the Racecourse near Government House. About mid-afternoon, Moore instructed Lieutenant-Colonel Rose, the CO 22 SAS, his Satellite Radio operator providing direct communications to London and Captain Bell to meet with General Menendez. After a safe route was agreed, a British helicopter flew the three from HMS *Fearless* to the soccer pitch behind Government House where Hussey confirmed Falklands Military Garrison had ordered 'Cease fire'. He then escorted the delegation to the Secretariat where Rose explained that London was demanding 'unconditional' surrender. Menendez said while he could instruct the Army, he had little influence over the Navy and Air Force and President Galtieri would have to order them.

In the middle of this tense and delicate situation, the journalist Max Hastings, of the *Evening Standard*, no doubt scenting a scoop, asked Brigadier Thompson if he could go forward, however, Thompson had more important matters to consider, namely reacting to the Argentine surrender and hardliners inciting unrest, and warned him that if he ran into a problems, he did not intend to risk the lives of his men with a rescue. Hobbling on a stick and wearing a civilian coat, Hastings walked past paras who assumed he was looking for a doctor. It was fortunate that 3rd Mechanised Infantry Regiment soldiers were defending the coast road viewed his arrival with suspicion and disbelief. A formal agreement had not been signed. A proud nation had been defeated and a response from officers and Special Forces was high and he would probably have been shot. Fortunately, he met a kindred spirit, a journalist named Eduardo Rotondo, and they exchanged photos. Although not the first to enter Stanley, his expedition has allowed Hastings to claim he was.

Heavy snow was falling when General Moore arrived by helicopter at the Secretariat at about 7 p.m. (Local). Conscious that London was demanding 'unconditional surrender', Moore believed this could tempt Argentine hardliners into refusing to surrender. Moore and Menendez signed the Instrument of Surrender behind closed doors in which Menendez crossed out 'unconditional' surrender of only all Argentine forces on East and West Falklands and the outlying British islands occupied by Argentina. A ceasefire was declared. To avoid confusion over the different time zones, both parties agreed the Instrument come into force at 23.59 GMT (9.59 p.m. local) on 14 June 1982. As part of the agreement, Argentine units could retain their Colours.

Next day, 3 Commando Brigade established Brigade HQ in the Secretariat and used its Northern Ireland experience to impose a security regime. The seventy-four-day occupation was over. Mr John Smith was drinking tea in West Store when Major-General Moore entered and said with masterly aplomb, 'Hello, I'm Jeremy Moore and I'm sorry it took us three weeks to get here'.

HQ Land Forces faced a major humanitarian problem of supporting a population shocked by occupation and liberation, repatriating 10,000 prisoners, many in a poor state of health, and making safe munitions and disposing of guns and equipment. There were no lights in Stanley for several days. The Commando Brigade Intelligence immediately searched Government House, the Secretariat and Argentine headquarters for information. The arrival of HQ Land Forces and 5th Brigade intelligence allowed a counter-intelligence operation to investigate the extent of Argentine espionage, subversion and collaboration. Several defectors from a Polish fish factory ship were interviewed. Several Argentines resident in Stanley had been evacuated to Argentina. That Argentine officers were permitted to keep sidearms, apparently to defend themselves against the anger of their men, was not appreciated and a discreet operation was mounted to disarm officers. The ever-present ICRC monitored the transfer of several hundred wounded and ill from a warehouse used as a field hospital to the *Almirante Irizar*. Arrangements were made to release Flight-Lieutenant Glover in Argentina and the SAS sergeant captured on West Falkland.

An Argentine brigadier-general was briefed that prisoners were to be assembled at Stanley Airport and would to be repatriated as soon as possible. They were to be fed under his arrangements from several unopened shipping containers full of food and twenty-four-hour ration boxes containing a small bottle of Scotch whisky. He was not informed that 600 officers were to be retained until Argentina surrendered 'unconditionally', for example senior officers, intelligence, military police, radar and communications technicians, journalists and of intelligence interest

Repatriation began the night after the surrender when the *Canberra* embarked with the first consignment of about 4,000 prisoners in an operation that took about eighteen hours. A simple routine emerged of columns of about 200 prisoners being escorted to the Public Jetty where the Intelligence check point interrogated every prisoner and selected those to be retained as Special Category and sent to the Ajax Bay prison camp to join those who had been captured in the fighting. It was during these interviews that accounts of the widespread use of field punishments emerged. Several officers masquerading as other ranks were betrayed by conscripts. About twenty large Alsatian war dogs unable to 'woof' in English were repatriated with their handlers. The Royal Military Police and Royal Marines Police then searched and removed all equipment except for a spoon.

The prisoners were searched again on boarding the *Canberra* by the Commando Forces Band before being allocated cabins and fed. The conscripts appreciated the friendliness on the ships that repatriated them to Argentina. The same selection process was also applied to prisoners at Ajax Bay and on West Falklands. Prisoners awaiting selection were formed into working parties that assembled the paraphernalia of the defeated army of weapons, vehicles, artillery and equipment and cleared the streets of Stanley of live and spent ammunition. Those with appropriate skills helped repair essential services. The senior Argentine military engineer handed over maps of minefields and defences and about thirty-five engineers accepted parole to work with the Royal Engineers and defuse mines and booby traps. Within the week, the Falklands was largely empty of prisoners.

Meanwhile, a small naval task force that included a troop from M Company, 42 Commando, recaptured Thule from a small Argentine military presence on 19 June amid snow, whiteout and a fierce windchill. This completed the recapture of British interests in the South Atlantic region.

Within the week of the surrender, 3 Commando Brigade embarked on the *Canberra* and other ships sailed for UK. The *Canberra* arrived at Southampton on 11 July to an unexpected welcome from families on the jetty and from the public. 5th Infantry Brigade remained as the garrison until relieved. Next day, Argentina unconditionally surrendered and the 593 Special Category prisoners and others at Ajax Bay transferred to the requisitioned Roll-on/Roll-off ferry *St Edmund* were formally released at Port Madryn. The war was over.

Argentina continues to grumble. Alexander Betts (1947–2020), a third generation Falkland Islander sympathetic to Argentina, claimed he was exiled by the British forces. He abandoned his family to live in Argentina where, with other pro-*Malvinas*, he promoted the claim at the United Nations Special Committee of Decolonisation. Appointed as an advisor of the Tierra del Fuego *Malvinas* Observatory, he controversially accepted an Argentine war pension because he had been on the islands during the war.

161 British were killed or died of wounds, namely ninety Royal Navy, twenty-seven Royal Marines, 123 Army, one RAF, eight Royal Fleet Auxiliary, nine Merchant Navy and three women. Included in Merchant Navy was an officer who died from medical complications and two Royal Navy died of wounds after being transferred to UK.

Of those not buried at sea, thirteen are buried in the San Carlos War Cemetery, a Royal Navy pilot is buried near Goose Green, a SAS captain at Port Howard and the women are at Stanley. Most of those returned to UK were interred under family arrangements. 777 British were wounded.

Regrettably, matters relating to Argentine casualties became stuck within national politics. In July 1982, of the 1,366 casualties declared by the Argentine Defence Ministry, 156 soldiers, 53 airman, 323 sailors and 105 were missing. 883 were wounded, 222 ill and 34 were treated for malnutrition.

When Captain Geoffrey Cardozo was posted to the Falklands in mid-1982 for a six-month tour to investigate post-traumatic stress, most of the Argentine dead had been left on the battlefields where they died. Claiming they were already 'at home', Argentina rejected an offer from Great Britain to repatriate them. Cardozo began to identify the casualties and even though many lacked 'dog tags', personal effects proved helpful in identification. Those who could not be identified were wrapped in three layers of sheets, plastic and PVC bags, placed in wooden coffins with any property and given a Christian burial marked by a white wooden cross and *Soldado Argentino Solo Conocido Por Dios* ('Argentine Soldier Known Only By God'). Royal Engineers clearing minefields proved useful contacts. When the British Government funded a project for an Argentine war cemetery in December 1982, Brooke Hardcastle donated land at Darwin and Cardozo was appointed to lead the project and the Commonwealth War Graves Commission helped design and construct the cemetery. Throughout, information was shared with the ICRC and Argentina. In due course, Cardozo linked up with former conscript Julio Aro who had formed the *No Me Olvides* (Don't Forget Me) charity to help commemorate the Argentine dead. 300 relatives made the first pilgrimage to Darwin when the ICRC organised the first Argentine family visit in 1991.

Casualties from mine clearing the battlefields led the British Government to cease operations and sign the 2007 Ottawa Treaty (Anti-Personnel Mine Ban Convention). Two years later, the Foreign & Commonwealth Office financed Safeline Global Ltd to continue the work. A senior manager was John Hare, formerly 9th Parachute Engineer Squadron and seriously wounded at Port San Carlos on 23 May 1982 in the 3 Para 'blue on blue'. The de-miners, mainly Zimbabwean, hand-lifted mines and operated armoured machinery trawling the sand dunes and overgrown and flooded ground. In November 2020, forty years after the end of war, Safeline had cleared approximately 21 million square metres.

In UK, the 1983 Franks Committee cleared the Government of Prime Minister Thatcher of not forecasting the Junta's 'unprovoked aggression'. Recommendations about the collection and use of intelligence led to the creation of the Joint Intelligence Committee. The two volumes of *The Official History of the Falklands Campaign* by Sir Lawrence Freedman describes the war.

In Argentina, the National Reorganisation Process, acceptance of criminality during the 'Dirty War', the discarding of parliamentary democracy and attempts by the Junta to shield the defeat was undermined in December 1983 by the Calvi Report. Assembled from interviews of officers, non-commissioned officers and other ranks, reports of commanding officers and documents smuggled onto the *Almirante Irízar,* then designated as a hospital ship, it exposed the inter-service political rivalry'. While the Marines were provided to fight a small war, the Army was not trained, nor equipped and not prepared to fight the war. There was a lack of commitment from the Navy and the Air Force to support the Army. Daniel Kon in his *The Boys of the War* interviewed conscripts claiming they had no idea why they are at war and officers were so inefficient that hungry soldiers stole food from military depots. Among several officers who were either imprisoned or placed under house arrest, Lieutenant-Commander Astiz, captured at South Georgia and wanted by Sweden and France, was taken to UK; however, British law in 1982 concluded he had not committed any offences against British nationals and there was no case to answer. He was repatriated on 10 June 1982 and was later convicted and imprisoned for life. At least the soccer forward Diego Maradona raised Argentine morale when he scored against England in the 1986 Football World Cup by tapping the ball into the net.

The Falklands is a prosperous and welcoming community that offers a range of activities to visitors. Fishing has enhanced economic progress and oil reserves are being researched. British regional interests and security are defended by the British Forces South Atlantic Islands of a garrison and airbase at Mount Pleasant on West Falkland and the nautical Protection Zone patrolled by the Royal Navy Atlantic Patrol.

# Bibliography

**Great Britain**

Bound, Graham, *Invasion 1982, The Falkland Islanders' Story* (Pen & Sword (Military)) (2002)

Pugh, Nicci; *White Ship-Red Crosses: A Nursing Memoir of the Falklands War* (Melrose Books, 2012)

**Argentina**

Moro, Rubin Oscar, *La Trampa de Malvinas: Historia Del Conflicto del Atlantico Sur* (Falklands Trap, History of the War in the South Atlantic, self-publication, 2005).

Ramos, Javier, *Isla Bourbon: El Equipo de Combate Montalvo en Malvinas* (No. 3 Marine Infantry Battalion detachment – Pebble Island).